"With all thy getting, get understanding"

—B.C. FORBES

Forbes @100

THE PAST, THE PRESENT—AND THE FUTURE,
FROM THE 100 GREATEST LIVING BUSINESS MINDS

EDITED BY RANDALL LANE • FOREWORD BY STEVE FORBES • PHOTOGRAPHY BY MARTIN SCHOELLER

Copyright © 2017 by ForbesMedia.

All Photographs Copyright @2017 by Martin Schoeller

All rights reserved. No part of this book may be used or reproduced in any manner whatsoever without prior written consent of the author, except as provided by the United States of America copyright law.

Published by ForbesBooks, Charleston, South Carolina.
Member of Advantage Media Group.

ForbesBooks is a registered trademark, and the ForbesBooks colophon is a trademark of Forbes Media, LLC.

Printed and bound in Iceland.

Photographs by Martin Schoeller
Producer: Lisa Hooper
First Photo Assistant and Retouching: Lauren Juratovac
Retouching: Jill Lewis
Photo Assistant: Jan Düfelsiek

ISBN: 978-1-946633-22-4
LCCN: 2017954098

INTRODUCTION

IN AN ERA OF medical breakthroughs and disruptive business models, a media company hitting the century mark seems even more impressive than a human doing so. How has *Forbes* survived, and thrived, all these years? Initial credit belongs to founder B.C. Forbes, who popularized the idea that chronicling business meant chronicling *people* rather than faceless corporations. Further credit goes to Malcolm Forbes, who imbued the *Forbes* brand with a quality—success—that will never go out of style; and to *Forbes'* influential editor of the last half of the twentieth century, Jim Michaels, who embraced the idea of the magazine as the "drama critic of capitalism," with a bold, opinionated voice that leverages thorough reporting in order to call it like we see it.

The fact that our first 100 years coincided with the same century that proved the primacy of capitalism and free markets over communism and state-controlled economic models didn't hurt either.

You'll see these notes repeat as our history unwinds, page by page. It would be a shame, however, to waste a momentous anniversary by spending too much time looking back. *Forbes* has always looked forward, and that's what the bulk of this book does as well, with the 100 greatest business minds of the present offering their 100 greatest lessons and ideas for the future. We believe this is the greatest-ever amalgamation of business essays, as well as the greatest-ever portrait portfolio of business leaders (all shot by one photographer, the great Martin Schoeller, who literally traveled around the world to create a unified photo package for us).

As with any major *Forbes* project, this required serious collaboration. Michael Solomon was instrumental in cobbling together the 100 years of our history, and Michael Noer, Matt Schifrin, Abram Brown, Alexandra Wilson, Brian Dawson and Sue Radlauer all played critical roles in this project. In terms of delivering these essays, additional credit goes to the talented group of Susan Adams, Dan Alexander, George Anders, Madeline Berg, Steven Bertoni, Kathleen Chaykowski, Kerry A. Dolan, Matt Drange, Antoine Gara, Zack O'Malley Greenburg, Miguel Helft, Chris Helman, Matthew Herper, Alex Konrad, Luisa Kroll, Janet Novack, Clare O'Connor, Michael Ozanian, Natalie Robehmed, Halah Touryalai and Nathan Vardi.

Our design and photography team, led by Bob Mansfield, did terrific work to create the most visually impressive project of our entire first century. In addition to Martin Schoeller and Robyn Selman, thank you to Charles Brucaliere, Anton Klusener, Dan Hennessy, Matt Herrmann and Lisa Hooper.

This book went from idea to actuality because of the creativity and determination of Tom Davis and Liz Walsh. *Forbes'* leadership team fully supported this project, along with so many other great initiatives around our centennial, with particular appreciation to Mike Perlis, Mike Federle, Mark Howard, Mike York, Nina LaFrance, Mia Carbonell and our chief product officer, Lewis D'Vorkin, who does so much to keep our editorial model constantly evolving and innovating.

It's somewhat ironic that a media company like *Forbes,* so keen to try new things, would have as its ultimate centennial keepsake a printed coffee-table book. But it's also a reflection of what makes *Forbes* special: a worldview that doesn't bend with the wind, but instead provides sturdiness and timelessness in an era that demands more of both.

Randall Lane
Editor, *Forbes* Magazine

THE NEXT 100 YEARS (WE'RE JUST GETTING STARTED)

WE'RE IMMENSELY PROUD of *Forbes*' legacy. For a solid century, we've championed free-market capitalism and the power of entrepreneurs in the United States and around the world. Our remit has always been to tell stories of business success: how people achieve it, and what they do with it once they have it.

That mission will remain our animating force as we move into our next 100 years. Through time, we've always been a powerful voice of media leadership and innovation; our hard-won business-journalism credibility has been the project of many decades, and of talented individuals too numerous to count.

In recent years especially we've embraced digital and mobile opportunities as few established companies have, increasing our audience by orders of magnitude. We now reach more business hearts and minds than ever, fostering a dialogue that's immediate, informed, diverse and influential—in the process becoming a great media company that's also a nimble, technology-driven business.

As we grow, we've invested in the future by betting on today's most promising young entrepreneurs. Our 30 Under 30 franchise has connected *Forbes* to the future of business and innovation worldwide. The intimate relationships we're building with tomorrow's leaders is just one edge certain to power our next century of success.

A brand as iconic as *Forbes* can and will—indeed, must—go far beyond media. We have ambitious initiatives on tap in events, research, education, travel, real estate, online commerce, financial services and more that will blossom into major businesses in the years (and decades) ahead. Everything we do is propelled by our sun-never-sets media network that, as of this writing, extends its reach to 38 countries. Our future, like the future of commerce itself, will be increasingly global, and strategic investment from Asia gives us an exciting advantage in this ever-more-important region.

No one could have predicted the last hundred years, an illuminating overview of which you'll find in the pages to come. Whatever lies ahead, we're ready—chests out and sights trained on the future of business around the world. Here's to the next 100—we've only just begun.

Mike Perlis
CEO and Executive Chairman, Forbes Media

OUR FIRST 100 YEARS

BY STEVE FORBES, EDITOR-IN-CHIEF

THE YEAR OF *Forbes*' founding, 1917, was one of the most momentous in history. The U.S. entered the Great War, a dramatic break from our isolationist tradition. The October Communist coup in Russia brought into power the first modern totalitarian regime, one which would violently challenge the very existence of capitalism and the liberal democratic order.

To launch a new publication in the midst of a world war would strike most as folly. But B.C. Forbes, the sixth of ten children of a Scottish tailor, had long burned with ambition to become a business writer and, ultimately, his own boss. He first went to South Africa, where he worked for the editor of the new *Rand Daily Mail*, Edgar Wallace, who later achieved fame in Britain and the U.S. as a novelist. Many a time B.C. found himself writing editorials for his oft-inebriated boss. But South Africa was too small a pond, and in 1904 B.C. immigrated to the U.S. Landing in New York, he had a hard time getting a job, but instead of going home B.C. decided to offer his services to an editor for free for several weeks to "prove my worth." He had no idea whether he would be tossed out when, after the allotted time, he would ask for a salary, but like any entrepreneur, he knew that doing things the "normal" way would get him nowhere. He got the job. Full of energy, B.C. assumed a nom de plume and, at the same time, obtained a job with another publication, also as a business writer. Legend has it that the two editors later got into an argument over who had the better business reporter—it was B.C. in both cases.

B.C. became a nationally renowned financial writer, not only reporting and turning out a syndicated column but also authoring books. Yet, instead of just writing about individuals who started their own firms, he itched to start one himself. And being a Scotsman, B.C. hated not using all the material he gathered. (He would have loved being able to blog to his heart's content.) He felt the time had come to start his own publication. It was originally titled *Doers and Doings*, but B.C. was persuaded to use his surname, a not-uncommon practice in those days.

B.C. Forbes deeply believed in what we today call entrepreneurial capitalism. He loved chronicling the doings of business leaders—the bolder, the better. He was no apologist, however. He railed against those he felt were abusing employees or were incompetently managing their firms. He stated in the first issue of *Forbes*, "Business was originated to produce happiness, not to pile up millions." He had no truck with the notion that we are ultimately governed by impersonal forces.

Forbes boomed during the 1920s. William Randolph Hearst, the media mogul who was the model for Orson Welles' classic film *Citizen Kane*, offered to buy B.C.'s creation in 1928 for what today would be the equivalent of tens of millions of dollars. B.C. proudly turned him down. He soon had cause to wonder if he had made a catastrophic mistake.

Forbes was hit hard by the Depression. By 1932, the company was bankrupt in all but name, as advertising had contracted more than 80%. B.C. kept his creation alive through his freelance earnings—he was still a columnist for the Hearst papers—and by instituting what was dubbed "Scotch week": Every fourth week employees went without a paycheck, which meant a 25% pay cut. But in those desperate times people were happy just to have a job. B.C. himself didn't cash any of his paychecks for several years.

Barely surviving the Depression, *Forbes* limped along during the 1930s, overshadowed by *BusinessWeek* (owned then by McGraw-Hill) and *Fortune* (Time Inc.). In 1945, B.C.'s son Malcolm (MSF) joined *Forbes* after being discharged from the Army, where he'd been badly wounded while serving as a machine-gunner. Another son, Bruce, was already at the company.

At the time *Forbes*' content was mostly made up of freelance pieces. MSF began the process of hiring full-time editorial staffers, rightly believing that this would dramatically improve the editorial product. He also launched *The Forbes Investor*, a weekly newsletter that recommended stocks and analyzed the previous week's market news. The price of the newsletter was an outlandish $35 a year (*Forbes* subscriptions went for $4 or less), with production costs a fraction of the magazine's. The newsletter was an instant success and provided the capital to reorganize the company.

In 1947 *Forbes* marked its 30th anniversary and nascent revival with a major dinner at New York's Waldorf Astoria. New York governor Thomas Dewey gave the evening's major address, and he didn't disappoint, making headlines by declaring his intention to run for President in 1948. (Although he was heavily favored to win—*Life* magazine ran a photograph of Dewey with the caption "The next President travels by ferry boat over the broad waters of San Francisco Bay" before the election—Dewey lost to incumbent Harry Truman in America's greatest electoral upset prior to Donald Trump's stunning 2016 victory.)

Editorial content improved, as did circulation and advertising with a number of innovations. In January 1949 *Forbes* introduced what would become its annual report card on industries and companies, thereby starting the buildup of its statistical muscle. January traditionally was the deadest month of the year for advertising, but with this issue's advent it became one of the best. In the 1950s the magazine began in-depth coverage of the burgeoning mutual fund industry. Every year we would give each fund a letter grade for long-term performance in up markets and another in down markets. Despite bitter memories of the Depression, millions of people were starting to invest again as their economic conditions got better.

The longtime (1961–99), brilliant, crusty, cowed-by-no-one editor James Michaels did more than anyone else to bring about *Forbes*' editorial prominence. We developed a reputation for hard-hitting stories that evaluate companies the way critics

Key figures in the history of *Forbes*: founder B.C. and son Malcolm, as young men.

Ronald Reagan, SF and Mikhail Gorbachev at *Forbes'* 75th anniversary celebration. Theme: B.C. Forbes' creation outlasted Lenin's.

GLEN DAVIS

critique a stage play. What made these pieces ring true was our growing sophistication in digging into corporate balance sheets in a way that no other publication did. One example: a cover story in 1998 exposing the obscure and outrageous fees charged by most annuities, which made this popular vehicle a decidedly poor investment for customers.

The magazine's growing fame was accelerated in 1982 with the introduction of a special annual issue that ranked the 400 richest Americans. The idea was Malcolm's (the "400" number was inspired by the so-called 400 Ball hosted in 1892 by New York's social queen, Caroline Astor. Social arbiter Ward McAllister coined the phrase "The Four Hundred"). MSF met fierce internal resistance: How can we find out who these people are, since much of the necessary information isn't public? If we think someone might qualify, how can we dig up their finances? Anyway, won't our listing them make them targets for kidnappers, robbers and fundraisers? The editorial department conducted a "study" and told Malcolm his idea was absolutely unfeasible.

"Okay," the boss replied. "I'll take it out of your hands and do it myself; I'll hire some outside staff and raid a few of yours." Edit capitulated. In fact, the handful of editors and reporters involved on what was dubbed "The Rich List" deftly developed ways of getting seemingly unavailable information, and *Forbes* has been widening the search and refining the methods of mining data ever since. The first edition was a huge success, editorially and financially, and lists became a *Forbes* mainstay. The key was and is credibility and innovation. For example, *Forbes'* 30 Under 30, an annual list of 30 impressive young achievers in 20 different categories, has been phenomenally successful, thanks to Randall Lane, its originator and the editor of *Forbes*, and his editorial colleagues.

Key to *Forbes'* continued success was what we now call "branding." Having an ever better product isn't enough, as Steve Jobs vividly demonstrated with his almost manic emphasis on sleek and beautiful designs. In 1964, when MSF succeeded his brother Bruce, who had died of cancer at age 48, the company accelerated moves that would make *Forbes* synonymous worldwide with entrepreneurial achievement, success and the good life. MSF did things no traditional CEO would do: He put together the world's largest private collection of Imperial Easter Eggs created by the legendary Carl Fabergé for Russia's Czars and Czarinas and members of the Russian aristocracy. Hundreds of other Fabergé pieces were also added, as were other unusual works of art. Another of MSF's passions was collecting American presidential and historical letters, manuscripts and memorabilia. In the 1980s he built a museum on the ground floor of the Forbes Building on lower Fifth Avenue to house them all, as well as his collections of toy boats and toy soldiers—some of which were in moving dioramas, complete with rousing music—and opened the museum to the public.

MSF had always been interested in sailing, and so the company bought the first of *The Highlander*s in 1955—and then over the years had a succession of ever more lavish and exquisitely designed vessels built. Each was used extensively to woo advertising on all levels, from ad agency personnel to the CEOs of the world's largest corporations. From an early age, my siblings and I learned that these events had one ultimate goal: To secure ad dollars for *Forbes*—and we were all expected to help in this endeavor. Heads of state also came on board. In the 1980s Sec-

retary of State George Schultz used *The Highlander* to conduct secret negotiations between Israeli and Arab diplomats.

Impressive properties in the U.S. and around the world were acquired, and all were relentlessly used for marketing. MSF also became famous for his hot-air balloons and motorcycles. At Château de Balleroy, a Forbes property in France, the country in which hot-air ballooning originated, Malcolm hosted an annual ballooning festival that attracted outstanding balloon pilots from around the world. He always also brought in a number of journalists, CEOs and celebrities. Not only was there ballooning but also numerous amusement rides and food stalls, not to mention the fireworks at night. Thousands of people attended, with the festivals generating considerable international press coverage.

Elaborate luncheons for CEOs were a routine in the brownstone house connected to the Forbes company headquarters. Each guest was given an advertising pitch before leaving. A Tiffany-made silver cup, inscribed with the person's name and the date of the luncheon and embossed on the bottom with a Forbes stag's head, would subsequently be sent to each guest, along with the information that another such cup with the same inscription would hang in the brownstone's wine cellar, entitling the guest to come by anytime to try the wine. None ever did.

The good feelings garnered from this kind of entertainment, however, didn't always endure. Malcolm once invited a railroad CEO to lunch with whom he'd been exchanging barbs. It was time to bury the hatchet! The affair went well, but a few months later the magazine hit him again. The furious executive sent the cup back.

In 1967 *Forbes* finally surpassed the number of advertising pages it had run in 1929. To mark its 50th birthday, MSF threw a spectacular party at his New Jersey home. More than 500 leaders of America's mightiest corporations and their spouses attended. The keynote address was delivered by Vice President Hubert Humphrey, a very liberal Democrat. But Humphrey won over the crowd with humor and the theme that government and business need not be enemies. (Malcolm had come to know Humphrey several years before and had written a glowing Fact & Comment editorial about him in early 1964. Humphrey subsequently told Malcolm that the piece had helped persuade President Lyndon Johnson to choose Humphrey as his running mate.)

Forbes also celebrated its 70th anniversary at MSF's New Jersey home. Guests still remember the 70 bagpipers marching down a hill, seemingly coming out of the mists of the nearby woods. Scores of helicopters had ferried in the corporate moguls. No surprise, the largest chopper belonged to Donald Trump.

Such events didn't meet with universal approbation. In August 1989 MSF gave a party in Tangier, Morocco, to mark his 70th birthday at Palais Mendoub, which Forbes had purchased years before (now, fittingly, owned by the king of Morocco). In chartered aircraft, including a supersonic Concorde, he flew in 1,000 corporate moguls and their spouses, celebrities—including his date, Elizabeth Taylor—key *Forbes* colleagues, personal friends and members of the media. It was quite the bash, with a fabulous fireworks extravaganza that easily outdid Macy's legendary Fourth of July displays in NYC. The following morning guests were treated to an extraordinary exhibition of the king's special horsemen, whose steads galloped down the field at a roaring pace—as their riders fired their rifles into the air and reloaded—then stopped on a dime and turned to repeat the process. Even though MSF personally footed the bills for this affair, he was excoriated in certain parts of the media at home—a lot of people are never short on ideas of how to spend other people's money. To some outsiders, all of this looked like wasteful extravagance. It was the opposite: It created a global image for *Forbes* that is as powerful today as it was decades ago. Many businesspeople and entertainers regard landing on the cover of *Forbes* as the ultimate proof of their achievements. Talk about branding!

Although Forbes Inc. was a fraction of the size of such media powerhouses as Time, Dow Jones and McGraw-Hill, its reputation was bigger, more prestigious and more glamorous. The magazine surpassed rivals, *Fortune* and *BusinessWeek*, in the clout it exerted in the business world.

In 1992 *Forbes* observed its 75th anniversary with a major event at Radio City Music Hall. The highlight was addresses by former President Ronald Reagan, whose policies and adroit diplomacy had been crucial to the U.S. winning the Cold War, and Mikhail Gorbachev, the last leader of the recently defunct Soviet Union, which had been created in 1917, the same year as *Forbes*' founding. What a pairing! B.C. would have been proud his creation had outlasted Lenin's.

This delightful highlight almost didn't happen, however. Just before the pair were to go on stage, Gorbachev declared that he wasn't going to participate unless a series of last-minute demands were met, including his going on stage alone. We had repeatedly gone over the particulars of how the evening was to unfold with Gorbachev's people, and they had repeatedly agreed to everything. After a terrifying time, we calmed the former Soviet leader down, and the event went off splendidly. In his remarks, though, Gorbachev mentioned that Steve Forbes was a good capitalist because he had exploited Gorbachev. The audience laughed, thinking he was inserting some humor, particularly after Reagan had employed plenty of it in his speech. But we, who had been behind the scenes, knew differently— Gorbachev was dead serious!

The evening was capped off with an extraordinary documentary about the economic history of the 20th century and the triumph of Western-style, democratic capitalism over Soviet-style communism, entitled *Happily Ever After?* Thankfully, we had put in that question mark.

Forbes' post-WWII comeback and surge was in an industry whose fundamentals hadn't seen much change since the invention of the steam-powered rotary printing press in 1843, which had made the mass-marketing of newspapers and magazines possible. But with the ascension of the internet, the print world was being decimated.

It's a cliché to say, "You must reinvent yourself" or "Remake your company as if it were a startup." This is very difficult for legacy companies to do, which is why most eventually fall by the wayside. The mind is so accustomed to—and encumbered by—seeing the world and carrying out tasks in a set way. Even when managements do recognize industry-altering innovations coming at them and try to adjust, their responses are often too slow and unimaginative, or they go into panic mode. Think Kodak with the rise of digital photography.

In the mid-1990s most publishers thought that electronic publishing meant merely reproducing the printed page online. And just about every publisher was hesitant to make a commitment to fully developing their websites. Why give away their copy for free? Moreover, online advertising was then minuscule.

At the start of Forbes.com in 1996, we fortunately separated the online product from the magazine—different buildings, different staffs, different reporting lines. The new venture didn't just post what had appeared in the magazine; it also created a lot of original content, a true rarity for sites from legacy publishers. Forbes.com suffered considerable losses for several years before turning profitable. But the time eventually came when operations had to be combined. It was a cultural bloodbath, most particularly for the editorial departments. Print writers regarded their dot-com counterparts as peasants and poseurs, content to turn out plentiful but superficial and fourth-rate copy; the dot-com writers and editors saw print reporters and editors as lazy, overrated snobs.

My brother, Tim Forbes, who farsightedly recognized the impact the internet would have on the print world, played the indispensable role in navigating Forbes through these treacherous waters.

Big changes came in 2010 at Forbes with the arrival of Lewis D'Vorkin as chief product officer. Lewis had had a varied career in print, TV and high tech. He had been at *Forbes* during the 1990s and most recently had run his own startup, True/Slant, in which Forbes Inc. was a minority investor.

When Forbes, at Tim's behest, bought out Lewis' company, Lewis agreed to come on board. He had a daring and original vision of what the new online world of publishing should be. He created a new contributor model that today numbers some 1,700 experts in pertinent fields. Although having spent much of his professional life in the print world, Lewis didn't share the conceit that traditional journalism had a monopoly on discovering and purveying information for its audiences. If the content was good, who cared where it came from, including from advertisers? He boldly instituted what's called native advertising. Under Lewis' ceaseless prodding, his talented team is constantly developing new technologies and products that help readers and enhance their online experience. The challenges— and opportunities—are unending, including the new world of mobile devices, not to mention the advertising juggernauts of Google and Facebook. But, thanks to D'Vorkin and his crew, Forbes has been in the forefront. Also helping make the company's evolution to Forbes Media possible during this exciting time was the arrival in 2010 of Mike Perlis as CEO. Mike, who came from outside of Forbes, has a lifetime of publishing and startup experience.

Three years ago, Integrated Whale Media Investments, headed by T.C. Yam, bought a majority stake in Forbes, enabling the company to further expand on the digital side and to move into other areas. Today, *Forbes* editorial is stronger than ever.

What's ahead? Here's betting that in 2117 people will be infinitely richer with an unimaginably higher standard of living than that we enjoy today. And *Forbes*, if guided by the spirit of its founder, will be there to celebrate it.

Hot-air balloons, Moroccan horsemen, Fabergé eggs, *The Highlander*: MSF had a genius for branding.

A CENTURY OF FORBES

ISSUES OF *FORBES* from the past 100 years are individual snapshots of key moments in business (and world) history. Black Tuesday and the Great Depression. Renewed prosperity after the horrors of World War II. Communism versus capitalism in a decades-long battle of the biggest ideas of all. The emergence of high finance and the rise of the instant tech billionaire.

We begin, fittingly, in the pages of our first issue, September 15, 1917. From the beginning, *Forbes* featured stories of entrepreneurial capitalism and the people behind the world's greatest businesses—a focus that became the hallmark of *Forbes* in the century that followed.

Fool's Gould

George Jay Gould had mismanaged the railroad empire accumulated by his father while concentrating on building a "fairyland" estate, European vacations and polo. *Forbes* would later conclude that Gould "is impossible as the controlling power of railroads . . . in which the public have invested many millions of dollars."

The Rockefeller Quest

To complete a profile of John D. Rockefeller, B.C. Forbes studied both the oil industry and the man himself, interviewed his inner circle, including his son J.D. Jr., and even golfed with the billionaire at his Pocantico Hills estate, where Rockefeller "made good his threat to lick me," B.C. wrote.

Best Bosses

The relationship between employers and employees was the underpinning of "the peace and prosperity of the Republic." So *Forbes* ran an essay contest: "Who Is the Best Employer in America?" Winning pieces would get prize money, a total of $1,000 (about $20,000 today).

Business Rhapsody

It's doing your job the best you can
And being just to your fellow man;
It's making money—but holding friends.
And staying true to your aims and ends. . . .
It's serving, striving through strain and stress,
It's doing your Noblest—that's Success!

Wall Street Goes Over The Top

FINANCIERS AT THE FRONT: JUNE 1, 1918

FOURTEEN MONTHS AFTER America's entry into World War I, Wall Street had contributed men to the armed forces—B.C. Forbes walked through the emptied Bankers Trust Company Building and counted 490 away on the front lines—and men to sell the government bonds necessary to finance the war. "Brokers went the length of discouraging purchases in other securities and exhorting their customers to invest in the war loan," B.C. wrote in his cover story. By his calculation, no other industry was supplying more "free service" to the war effort.

Victory would arrive five months later, but not before America had raised $17 billion ($320 billion today) in five debt offerings while sending more than 1 million men off to Europe.

March 2, 1918
The First Rich List
"Newsboy to Multimillionaire"

January 11, 1919
"Is Humor a Business Asset?"

1918

1919

1920s

CRASH!: NOVEMBER 15, 1929

FROM AUGUST 1921 TO SEPTEMBER 1929, as America's easy-credit economy boomed, the stock market did, too. In that time the Dow Jones Industrial Average rose sixfold. When the U.S. skidded into recession in late 1929—due in part to lower steel production and reduced homebuilding—equities also plummeted. They began slipping on October 24 and continued their slide through October 29, "Black Tuesday." General Electric finished that day at $222 a share, having lost roughly half its market value from its high earlier in the year. Goodyear Tire nose-dived from $154 to $67. U.S. Steel shares, once more than $260, declined to $174.

Ever the contrarian, B.C. Forbes saw the carnage as an opportunity to buy. He had invested three-quarters of the money he had available after the crash and urged readers to follow: "I am willing to stake whatever reputation I may have . . . on this prediction: Good stocks purchased during this latest panic will net large profits."

Still, B.C. stopped well short of blind optimism. He concluded: "Now that the speculative orgy has ended, many who have been neglecting their legitimate business will return to their knitting. . . . This will be a good thing for the country. It cannot be expected, however, that prosperity will entirely escape the stock panic's aftermath."

August 7, 1920
"I read Forbes. I like it."
—Thomas Edison

October 29, 1921
"Is America Becoming Decadent?"

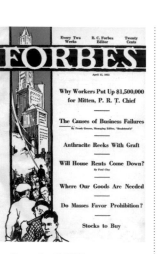

December 9, 1922
"The Story of a General Motors Giant"

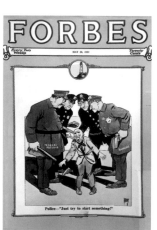

May 26, 1923
"The 25 Largest Banks in America"

November 15, 1924
"John Moody: How to Invest Profitably"

1920   **1921**   **1922**   **1923**   **1924**

EDISON'S ERROR: JUNE 15, 1929

ASKED IN 1929 to describe the current life stage of the electric age, its father, Thomas Edison, summed it up succinctly: "Yelling baby." In other words, it had a great future ahead of it—but a lot of growing up to do.

Edison went further and boldly forecast what he expected would happen when the industry matured a little. He believed that "mankind will draw electrical energy on a large scale directly from the sun." As Edison put it, "Man will always be able to create from nature as much power as he will need."

Scientists had been studying the core idea of solar power, the photoelectric effect, for the previous century; seven years earlier, Albert Einstein had won a Nobel Prize for his work on it. But Edison's prediction hasn't come true. It has been nearly 70 years since three Bell Labs scientists developed silicon photovoltaic cells—the first technology capable of converting sunlight into enough energy to power common electrical equipment—and still less than 1% of U.S. energy comes from the sun.

November 15, 1925
"The Wall Street Boom: How Long Will It Last?"

July 1, 1926
"Radio: What's Wrong With It?"

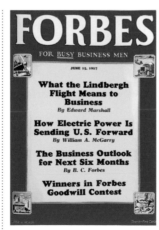

June 15, 1927
"What the Lindbergh Flight Means to Business"

December 1, 1928
"Selling 'Robots' Make Millions"

September 15, 1929
"Outlook for Stocks"

1925   1926   1927   1928   1929

1930s

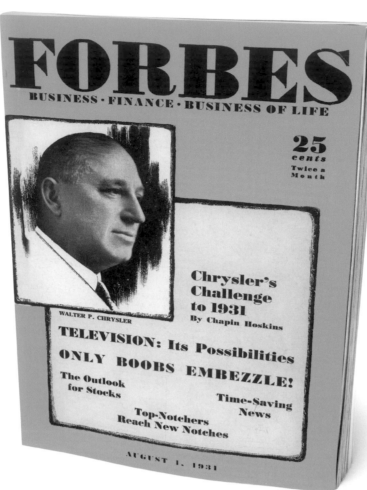

WALTER P. CHRYSLER

Chrysler's Challenge to 1931
By Chapin Hoskins

TELEVISION: Its Possibilities

ONLY BOOBS EMBEZZLE!

The Outlook for Stocks

Time-Saving News

Top-Notchers Reach New Notches

AUGUST 1, 1931

DRIVING FORCE: JULY 15, 1931

WALTER P. CHRYSLER faced a crisis: Nineteen thirty-one was the worst year for business since the invention of the automobile.

Chrysler responded by doubling down on a burgeoning area of his empire: the lower-priced Plymouth line he had introduced three years earlier. Chrysler advertisements of the time heralded the new 1931 Plymouth as "floating power" with "the smoothness of an eight [cylinder] . . . the economy of a four." A four-door, three-window sedan started at $635, or roughly $10,300 in today's dollars.

Chrysler instructed his company to embark on a new training program for dealers to ensure they understood the vehicle—and could sell it well. The regimen included an educational film that showed the Plymouth traversing the "worst roads in the United States," in Death Valley, where the temperature regularly tops 130 degrees.

January 1, 1930
"What Caused the Panic?"

December 1, 1931
"How California Keeps Men at Work"

November 1, 1932
15th Anniversary Issue
"Recovery and Reconstruction"

September 1, 1933
"What of Labor? Profits? Under the NRA?"

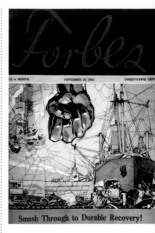

November 15, 1934
"Smash Through to Durable Recovery!"

1930   1931   1932   1933   1934

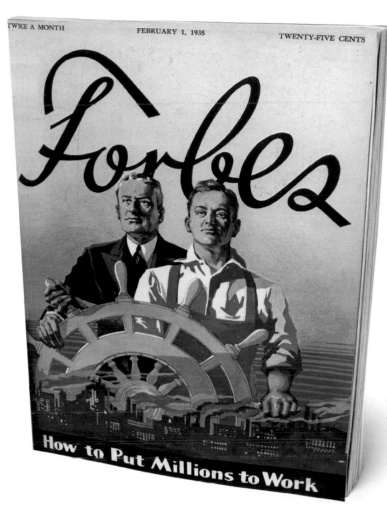

AMERICA'S SECRET STRENGTH: FEBRUARY 1, 1935

AMERICA WAS FIVE years into the Great Depression. Ten million people, roughly 20% of the workforce, were unemployed. The stock market was down about 70% from its 1929 peak; GDP had contracted by roughly 35%.

B.C. Forbes hated Franklin Delano Roosevelt's New Deal and doubted that the government could solve the country's economic problems. He placed his faith instead in America's entrepreneurial spirit. "This nation is so fundamentally sound, so virile, so resourceful, so enterprising, so rich in natural resources and so blessed with inventive, enterprising, practical business brains that, despite everything, it will triumph over every political and other obstacle, and achieve in the not-distant future a more bountiful and widespread measure of prosperity."

January 15, 1935
"America's Prosperity Trail-Blazer!"

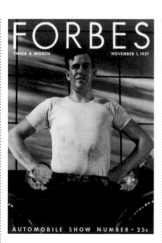

July 15, 1936
"Modernization Fills Lunch Boxes"

November 1, 1937
"The 1938 Cars"

June 15, 1938
"Electricity: Parade of Progress"

October 15, 1939
"How to Buy a Truck"

1935   **1936**   **1937**   **1938**   **1939**

1940s

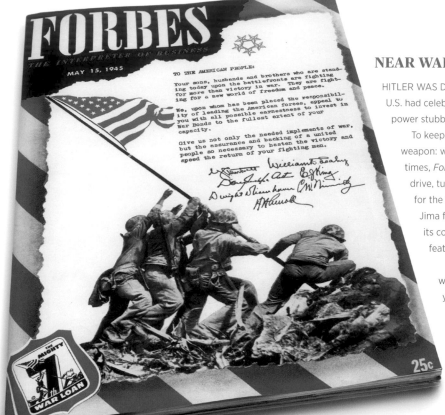

NEAR WAR'S END: MAY 15, 1945

HITLER WAS DEAD, and Mussolini, too, their forces defeated. The U.S. had celebrated victory in Europe a week earlier. But one Axis power stubbornly fought on: Japan.

To keep the effort going, America turned to a frequently used weapon: war bonds. In keeping with the patriotic spirit of the times, *Forbes* provided prime real estate to support the bond drive, turning its cover into a full-page unpaid advertisement for the 7th War Loan, complete with a glory shot of the Iwo Jima flag-raising. It wasn't the only time *Forbes* gave up its cover in this way: At least three others from the 1940s featured ads for war bonds.

For patriotic investors, $18.75 got them a $25 bond with Uncle Sam's promise to pay the difference ten years later. (In today's terms, that's $250 for $330 down the road.) In all, America would borrow $156 billion (roughly $2.1 trillion now) through war bonds.

October 15, 1940
"The West's New Gold Rush"

September 15, 1941
"Business in a New Era"

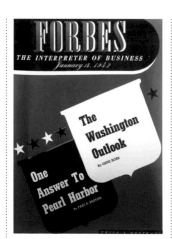

January 15, 1942
25th Anniversary Issue
"One Answer to Pearl Harbor"

May 15, 1943
First women on the cover
"Will the Girls Come Marching Home?"

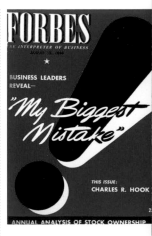

August 15, 1944
"Business Leaders Reveal—My Biggest Mistake"

1940   **1941**   **1942**   **1943**   **1944**

RED DAWN: AUGUST 1, 1946

AMERICA HAD DEFEATED the Nazis and Imperial Japan, but already had a new enemy: communism.

The country had a twofold fear: That communism might strike from abroad, backed by the U.S.S.R., or from within. Corporate bosses looked mistrustfully at blue-collar workers, unbound from the "no strike" pledge that kept factories open during World War II, and worried about red sympathizers.

Our story was penned by William J. Casey, a veteran of the Office of Strategic Services, America's wartime foreign intelligence service and CIA predecessor. He gave some sound advice to maintaining labor relations, such as quickly settling grievances. Yet some of it prefigured the hysteria that would culminate a few years later in McCarthyism. Casey offered up "Nine Ways to Spot a Communist," which included tracking workers' activities when they were off the clock to see if they attended rallies or meetings organized by known communists.

Casey would make a career out of being a fierce cold warrior—finally becoming CIA director under Ronald Reagan.

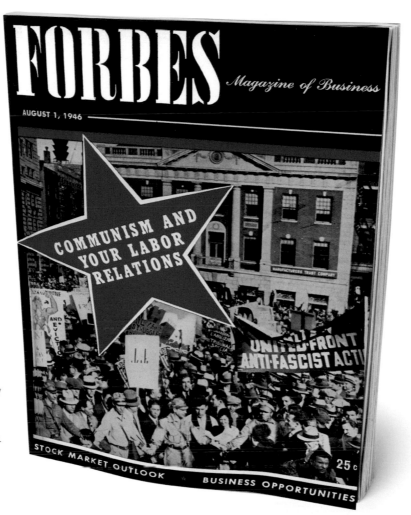

January 15, 1945
"Television Looks to the Future"

July 1, 1946
"Crack-Up in White Collar Morale!"

November 15, 1947
30th Anniversary Issue
"Today's 50 Foremost Business Leaders"

March 15, 1948
"Men of Achievement: Thomas J. Watson"

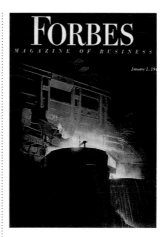

January 1, 1949
"Forbes' First Annual Report on American Industry"

| 1945 | 1946 | 1947 | 1948 | 1949 |

1950s

BLADES OF GLORY: NOVEMBER 15, 1952

TWO DECADES HAD passed since the death of King C. Gillette, but his razor manufacturer still ruled its industry. Half of the razors sold in America were Gillette, sales of which topped $100 million annually (over $900 million today). Company president Joseph Spang had run things smoothly for the previous 14 years, displaying the same knack for advertising and promotion as the business's legendary founder. Under Spang, Gillette's marketing budget had grown almost sevenfold to $7.5 million (about $70 million in 2017).

Gillette's business practices had some sharp edges, though. Its blue-collar employees described a highly stratified environment despite a professed egalitarian workplace. "We're peasants!" one told *Forbes*. The company didn't think too highly of its public shareholders, either, leaving investors to "ponder skeleton statements cloaked in consolidated mystery for 'competitive reasons.'"

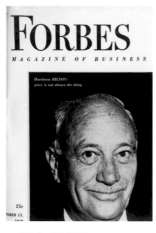

October 15, 1950
"Hotelman Hilton: Price Is Not Always the Thing"

january 15, 1951
"FTC's Mason: No Longer Chief Ogre"

October 1, 1952
35th Anniversary Issue
"Bertie Charles Forbes: Some Things Are Unconscionable"

February 15, 1953
"Paramount's Lamour and Hope: The Road to Mazuma Is Love"

March 15, 1954
"Planemakers' Yonder Is Still Up"

| 1950 | 1951 | 1952 | 1953 | 1954 |

MAN AND HIS MACHINES: JUNE 1, 1958

IN THE LATE 1950S the leading maker of "electronic brains"—ahem, computers—was IBM, with CEO Tom Watson Jr. at the helm. (His father, Tom Sr., who had run the company for almost 40 years, had died in 1956.) Junior had battled since the late '40s to convince Dad that computers would revolutionize business—particularly *their* business.

He won the argument, and as a result, IBM commanded 81% of the computer market and 89% of new orders. Sales had doubled since 1952 to $667 million (about $5.5 billion today). IBM's technology was impressive, as were the various accounting tricks Watson deployed to goose the company's cash flow—including tweaking the way IBM wrote off depreciated assets. Big Blue, eager to get even bigger, was hungry for cash: Its computers were too expensive for most companies to buy (the cheapest cost about $210,000 in current dollars), so it mostly rented them out—meaning large capital outlays and deferred revenue.

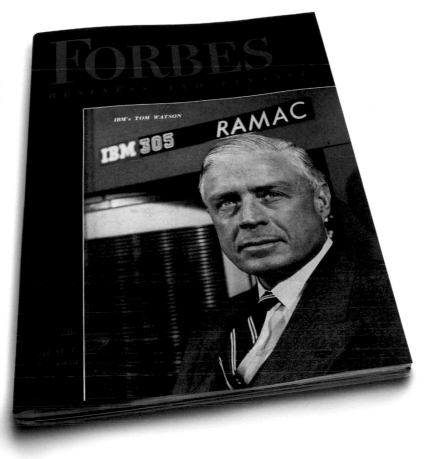

January 15, 1955
"Wall Street—Loaded Laggards"

October 1, 1956
"RCA's David Sarnoff"

September 15, 1957
40th Anniversary Issue
"General Telephone's Donald Power"

July 1, 1958
"Can Missiles Make Money?"

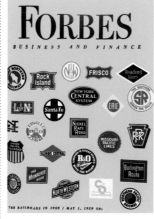

May 1, 1959
"The Railroads in 1959"

1955   1956   1957   1958   1959

1960s

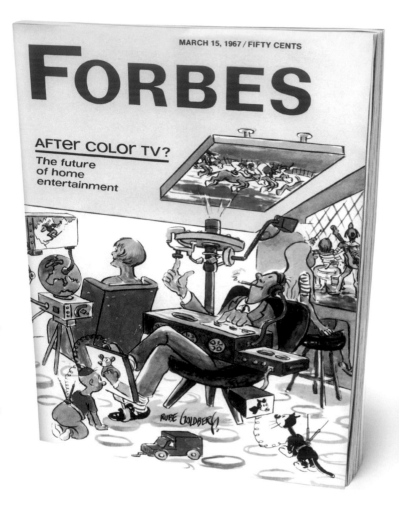

TUNED IN TO THE FUTURE: MARCH 15, 1967

"PRETTY SOON people won't be talking to people anymore. They'll be too busy
watching TV," predicted Rube Goldberg, the Pulitzer Prize-winning artist. At 83,
Goldberg came out of retirement to illustrate a *Forbes* cover about the rapidly
expanding industry of home-entertainment electronics.

Consumer spending on products such as televisions and stereos had doubled in
five years to $5 billion ($36 billion in 2016 dollars), and Kenneth Schwartz's story for
us sketched a future suggested by Goldberg's drawing. Schwartz offered a number
of sage predictions, including the advent of color videotape recorders, supersize
screens, and both cable and satellite TV. He also correctly anticipated on-demand
movies, shopping and information, essentially foreseeing smart televisions 45 years
before they became commonplace. Schwartz's forecast made only one real mistake:
that subscription-based TV wouldn't overtake commercial-supported television.

October 15, 1960
*"Wilmington, Delaware: Corporate
Capital of America"*

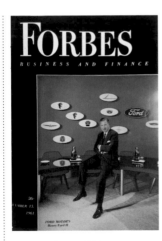

November 15, 1961
"Ford Motors' Henry Ford II"

May 1, 1962
"Clearer Skies Ahead for Airlines?"

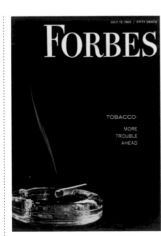

July 15, 1963
"Tobacco: More Trouble Ahead"

July 1, 1964
First woman on the cover
*"Seventh Avenue
Goes to Wall Street"*

1960   **1961**   **1962**   **1963**   **1964**

OCTOBER 1, 1969 / SIXTY CENTS

FORBES

The Newspaper Industry Going Modern, Going Public

PRINTING MONEY: OCTOBER 1, 1969

DESPITE THE ADVENT of television a couple decades earlier, the economics of newspaper publishing remained relentlessly, surprisingly golden. Conventional wisdom had predicted papers' demise, but as of late 1969 the industry had "never been healthier, not even in the heyday of Joseph Pulitzer and William Randolph Hearst."

TV had indeed generated more advertising spending than both magazines and radio since 1949. Yet newspapers still attracted far more: about $5.3 billion (some $37.7 billion today), more than one and a half times the amount spent on TV, thanks to the increased size of classified sections and new papers established in America's growing suburbs.

Although the industry for the most part remained privately owned by prominent local families, by the late 1960s it included several sizable publicly traded businesses, including Gannett— which published papers in 25 (mostly midsize) cities.

The future of print? "Profitable as newspapers are today, chances are they will be more profitable still in the years to come," our story concluded. That prediction held up—well, for 30 years, anyway, until the advent of the Web plunged newspapers into drum after drum of red ink.

April 1, 1965
"The $13-Billion Liquor Industry"

June 1, 1966
"Why Does College Cost So Much?"

April 1, 1967
"The Future of Electronic Money"

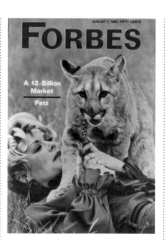

August 1, 1968
"A $2-Billion Market: Pets"

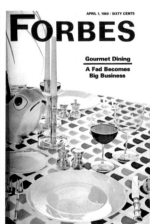

April 1, 1969
"Gourmet Dining: A Fad Becomes Big Business"

1965   1966   1967   1968   1969

FINANCING FANTASYLAND: MAY 1, 1971

FIVE MONTHS BEFORE Disney World's opening, the Walt Disney Co. was finishing its transformation of Florida swampland into a 27,000-acre theme park. It had a monorail, 300 doll-like animatronic children performing "It's a Small World" and two hotels—one reminiscent of a Polynesian resort, the other more modern, with a monorail stop in its 90-foot-high lobby.

Roy Disney had been charged with fulfilling his sibling's vision for a Florida park in the wake of Walt's death 11 years after Walt completed California's Disneyland in 1955. Roy built Disney World "by selling common stock and convertibles into a market that put a high and rising premium on Disney stock," which allowed Disney to pass "the inflationary costs on to the investing public."

In the end, the theme park cost some $320 million (close to $2 billion today), and Roy financed it without any long-term debt. He would, however, readily admit that the destination had cost about 40% more than originally forecast: "You just can't plan the cost of any darn thing these days."

MAY 1, 1971 / SEVENTY-FIVE CENTS

Will Walt Disney's Last Dream Come True?

October 1, 1970
"Nestle's Global Billions"

July 15, 1971
"Wall Street's New Fashions"

December 1, 1972
"Is Gillette Still Sharp?"

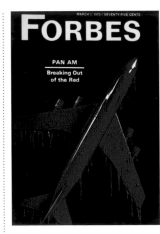

March 1, 1973
"Pan Am: Breaking Out of the Red"

August 15, 1974
"America's Saturated Cosmetics Market"

1970   **1971**   **1972**   **1973**   **1974**

GOLDEN SANDS: FEBRUARY 15, 1973

SIPPING CARDAMOM-flavored coffee in Saudi Arabia, *Forbes'* Stephen Quickel noticed how "Saudi men . . . go to their jobs in traditional Arab robes and headdress," while women donned full-length black veils. More startling were the kingdom's cane-wielding religious police, who "hustle off to the mosques anyone who shows signs of playing hooky" from services.

Just as apparent to Quickel: how rich Riyadh might become. By 1976, he estimated, the kingdom would pass the U.S. as the leading oil producer. Saudi Arabia had nearly quadruple America's proven reserves, and production had risen 27% to 5.7 million barrels a day from 1971 to 1972. Saudi oil revenue, Quickel figured, would soon hit $8 billion (roughly $43 billion today). Its wealth would then imbue it with "power that promises to be one of the most decisive—and potentially disruptive—forces in global economics for the balance of the century."

That October, Saudi-led OPEC imposed an oil embargo as punishment for America's having armed Israel during the Yom Kippur War. Oil skyrocketed—up 350% to $11.69 a barrel ($63 today) by January—and kept rising even after the embargo was lifted in March 1974, worsening U.S. inflation and overall economic woes.

March 15, 1975
"1975: A Time of Testing"

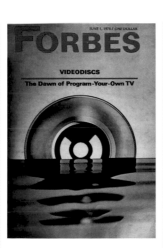

June 1, 1976
"Videodiscs: The Dawn of Program-Your-Own TV"

March 1, 1977
"MBA: The New Elite?"

October 30, 1978
"Immigration: Why the Lady Still Beckons

February 19, 1979
"Divorce: The High Cost of Breaking Up"

1975   **1976**   **1977**   **1978**   **1979**

1980s

WALL STREET'S WILD RIDE: NOVEMBER 19, 1984

THE FAST-MONEY ERA of the 1980s quickly came to resemble, well, a carousel. Seated on it were corporate raiders such as Victor Posner, Carl Lindner Jr. and the Belzberg brothers (Samuel and William). At its controls: Drexel Burnham Lambert's 38-year-old superstar, Michael Milken.

Milken's marvelous money machine ran on junk bonds—a $41.7 billion market ($96.7 billion in 2016 dollars) that had grown 340% in five years. He helped executives put together deals, and often those clients became investors in future Milken-led offerings. "Incestuous? That is one way of putting it," concluded the story's authors, Allan Sloan and Howard Rudnitsky. "There is nothing illegal about this. It is simply a case of one hand washing the other—to [everyone's] mutual profit."

The government disagreed. When a politically ambitious prosecutor named Rudy Giuliani needed a poster boy for the decade's excesses, he set his sights on Milken, who would plead guilty to fraud in 1990 and serve 22 months in prison. Since then Milken has devoted himself to philanthropy.

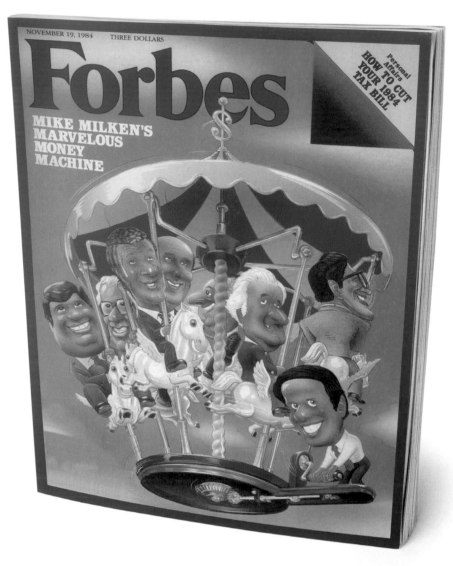

August 18, 1980
"Saddam Hussein: Can His Oil Billions Buy Leadership of the Arab World?"

August 3, 1981
"Are You Venture Capital Material?"

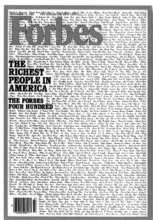

September 13, 1982
First Forbes 400
"The Richest People in America"

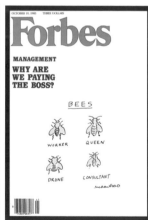

October 10, 1983
"Why Are We Paying the Boss?"

October 8, 1984
"These Days Everyone Is a Financial Planner"

1980   1981   1982   1983   1984

Forbes

JUNE 12, 1989

THREE DOLLARS SEVENTY-FIVE CENTS

ESTHER DYSON REPORTS FROM SOVIET COMPUTERLAND:

"LOADED WITH BRAINPOWER, BUT NO WAY TO HARNESS IT"

CYBER-SOVIETS: JUNE 12, 1989:

BEFORE RUSSIA GREW bold and sophisticated enough to hack a U.S. presidential election, the country's affinity for computers was evident even amid the collapse of the Soviet Union.

In the late 1980s, a growing group of entrepreneurial Russians ran computer-focused cooperatives, the private enterprises introduced under perestroika. They resold used Western computers, distributed Microsoft software and installed technology systems. They even wrote and marketed their own programs. Maxim Khomyakov, for instance, helped create an operating system called Chaos, a less-than-subtle poke at dysfunctional Soviet office life. It monitored the completion of paperwork and routine tasks and cost 50,000 rubles, or approximately $80,000 (roughly $160,000 in today's money).

"Computer hackers in the Western sense don't exist in the Soviet Union. Yet there exists a sizeable but indeterminate community of free spirits," concluded *Forbes'* Esther Dyson, daughter of noted English physicist Freeman Dyson and editor of Release 1.0, an influential newsletter on the emerging computer industry. "While the Soviets may lack the ability to use computer technology effectively, they are rich in fundamental . . . intelligence." Three decades later, it appears the hackers, not the entrepreneurs, reign supreme.

March 11, 1985
Corporate Takeovers: Why Is No One Safe?"

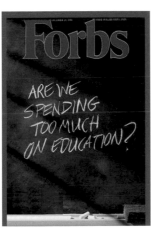

December 29, 1986
"Are We Spending Too Much on Education?"

July 13, 1987
70th Anniversary Issue
"Capitalism Is by Nature a Form of Change"

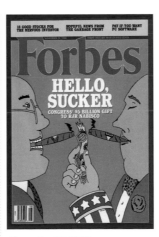

November 28, 1988
"How the Government Subsidizes Leveraged Takeovers"

December 25, 1989
"The Global Warming Panic"

1985   1986   1987   1988   1989

1990s

MADONNA
(1958–)
POP STAR

"She has just finished a rigorous song and dance routine in Nice, France. Madonna Ciccone, the 32-year-old bleached-blonde pop star, walks across the stage and pretends to rough up her background vocalists. Clad in an ivory-colored bustier and trousers from a business suit, Madonna then looks out at the crowd of 35,000 fans, grabs her crotch, raises her fist and yells, 'I'm the boss around here.' The crowd roars."
—*"A Brain for Sin and a Bod for Business" (October 1, 1990)*

CARLOS SLIM HELU
(1940–)
FOUNDER OF GRUPO CARSO (1980)

"Surrounded by paintings by Mexican artists and a collection of antique Mexican books and documents, Slim spends his mornings on the telephone and poring over figures, but he does not try to micromanage his far-flung holdings. Puffing on his ever-present Cuban cigar, he says, 'I can't be inside every company. My work is to think.'"
—*"El Conquistador" (September 16, 1991)*

MICHAEL JORDAN
(1963–)
BASKETBALL PLAYER

"No fool, Jordan knows he will have to put aside a good part of what he makes, because at 29 he isn't far from the end of his career. And he has expensive tastes to feed: He owns about a dozen cars (some from endorsements from Chicago area Chevrolet dealers) and an extensive wardrobe (thanks to a marketing venture that licenses the Jordan label). He is reportedly in the midst of constructing a 26,000-square-foot home in a Chicago suburb, where he lives with his wife and two young sons. Not that retirement from basketball will be the end of the line for Jordan."
— *"Put Them at Risk!" (May 25, 1992)*

DOUBTING THE DONALD: MAY 14, 1990

FOR MORE THAN 30 years, *Forbes* and Donald Trump have sparred over one recurring question: How much is he really worth? In 1990, that was especially relevant, as debt threatened to submerge his empire. Trump insisted his net worth was $4 billion or $5 billion— around $8 billion in today's dollars. Considering his mountain of debt, we figured he was worth a tenth of that—some $500 million (or roughly $930 million in current money). Trump hated the piece and wrote a syndicated newspaper column characterizing it as a "personal vendetta."

Still, the conclusion of *Forbes'* Richard L. Stern and John Connolly that "Donald Trump . . . may well remember 1990 as the toughest year of his life" was dead-on; that period was certainly an annus horribilis for the real estate mogul. His marriage to his first wife, Ivana, was having trouble, and he fell off *Forbes'* list of the world's billionaires. A year later, his recently opened Taj Mahal Casino wobbled into bankruptcy. It would be 1997 before he regained billionaire status.

March 19, 1990
"Malcolm Forbes: While Alive, He Lived"

April 1, 1991
"Microsoft's Bill Gates: Can Anyone Stop Him?"

March 2, 1992
"Country Conquers Rock"

May 10, 1993
"Can Henry Kravis' RJR Nabisco Survive Philip Morris' Price War?"

April 25, 1994
"Why Bill Clinton Looks Like a One-Termer"

TECH TITANS 1.0: JULY 27, 1998

AS A GROUP these 13 technocrats controlled vast wealth ($5.1 billion) and big businesses ($23 billion in total market value)—sums proportional to the disruption they had caused in almost every industry, from retail to sports, music to media. They had done it all via the then-new World Wide Web, and most of them, including Yahoo's Jerry Yang and Amazon.com's Jeff Bezos, had accomplished it before turning 40.

At the cover shoot "you could overhear them talking about potential business deals," *Forbes'* Eric Nee later recalled. "And kidding about stock prices: 'How's your stock do-ing?' 'What's your market cap now?'"

Within two years, of course, the internet bubble would burst, upending the best-laid plans of far more than just these Web pioneers. Several featured companies (Broadcom, Yahoo, CNET) survived. One thrived: Amazon, with $136 billion in sales, is today the world's fourth-most-valuable com-pany; Bezos is its second-richest person. Other firms and faces—remember Joseph Firmage's USWeb or Michael Levy's Sports-Line?—quickly faded.

December 18, 1995
"Businessman George Foreman"

March 11, 1996
"The Magician: George Lucas"

February 24, 1997
"Wall Street Sleaze: Bear, Stearns & the Bucket Shops"

March 9, 1998
"LBO Madness: The Hocus-Pocus Behind Those Fancy Deals"

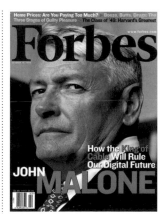

October 18, 1999
"John Malone: How the King of Cable Will Rule Our Digital Future"

1995   **1996**   **1997**   **1998**   **1999**

2000s

DIGITAL PITCHFORKS: NOVEMBER 14, 2005

AS THE WEB hit adolescence, it got, perhaps predictably, a great deal snottier. To wit: the exploding popularity, in the mid-2000s, of "Web logs," or blogs. When this issue of *Forbes* was published, Blogger.com, the leading plug-and-play platform for these new digital pamphlets, attracted 15 million visitors a month, more than the websites of the *New York Times*, *Washington Post* or *USA Today*. One subset of bloggers that drew our attention: those who shot to prominence tormenting big companies. "Blogs started a few years ago as a simple way for people to keep online diaries," wrote *Forbes*' Daniel Lyons, who would later put his reporting to use as a writer for HBO's *Silicon Valley*. "Suddenly they are the ultimate vehicle for brand-bashing, personal attacks, political extremism and smear campaigns."

Across America's C-suites, cold sweat moistened starched collars. "The potential for brand damage is really high," Frank Shaw, an executive at Microsoft's primary PR firm, Waggener Edstrom, told us. "There is bad information out there in the blog space, and you have only hours to get ahead of it and cut it off, especially if it's juicy." To meet this new demand, up popped firms like Intelliseek, a Cincinnati company that combed millions of blogs for clients such as P&G and Ford. "Bloggers . . . are only going to get more toxic," said Peter Blackshaw, Intelliseek's chief marketing officer. "This is the new reality."

He was more right than he probably ever imagined. The number of Web users worldwide is now over 3 billion, more than triple the number in 2005. And of course social media—Facebook alone has more than 2 billion users—has made it far easier to attack a corporate target. Circa 2017, a CEO being pummeled by a withering tweetstorm might actually look back on the mid-aughts as the good old days.

May 1, 2000
"Pierre Omidyar: The Dot-Com World Takes On the Charity Establishment"

October 15, 2001
"Life During Wartime: Fighting Back, Coping and Rebuilding"

December 23, 2002
85th Anniversary Issue
"85 Innovations That Changed the Way We Live"

March 3, 2003
"DreamWorks: Hollywood's Hottest Studio—Here Comes the Sequel"

October 4, 2004
"Phishing: The Net's Biggest Scam"

2000   **2001**   **2002**   **2003**   **2004**

AMERICAN CARNAGE: NOVEMBER 10, 2008

THINGS LOOKED BLEAK. Debris littered Wall Street: Markets convulsed, sickened by uncertainty and outright fear. Lehman Brothers, founded a decade before the Civil War, had gone bankrupt; Merrill Lynch desperately sold itself to Bank of America. Consumer confidence plummeted to its lowest since the measure was first recorded in 1967.

In Washington, the Bush administration and Congress had hammered together a $700 billion Rube Goldberg bank bailout—the fabled Troubled Asset Relief Program, or TARP—which was only the beginning of the government's efforts to prop up the listing economy, a project that would continue under the newly elected Barack Obama.

In *Forbes*, meanwhile, Editor-in-Chief Steve Forbes channeled the spirit of his all-hands-on-deck grandfather in 1929, outlining a plan for what might help an anxious nation bandage its economic wounds. Forbes advocated for cutting taxes, for "sensible, not punitive regulations in the financial sector," breaking up federal housing behemoths Fannie Mae and Freddie Mac, tying the hands of the Federal Reserve and linking the dollar to the price of gold at a range between $500 and $550. "If we have the kind of policies that marked the 1980s and not the kind that marked the 1930s and the 1970s, we will be in for a dazzling era of innovation and economic advances," Forbes wrote. "Free-market capitalism will save us—if we let it."

Not all his advice found receptive ears: Fan and Fred still stalk the earth, and the gold standard remains locked in a vault somewhere in Richard Nixon's presidential museum. But the fitful recovery the U.S. has witnessed since the depths of the crisis points to perhaps the American economy's most salient feature: its resilience. Capitalism, as it always does, survived to see another day.

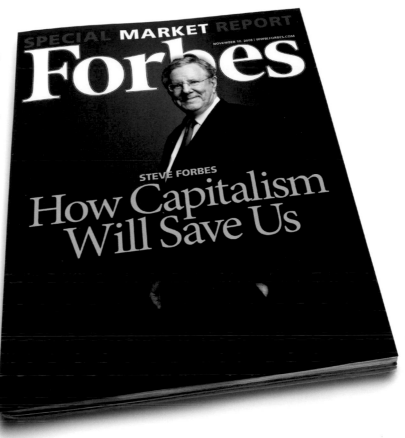

SPECIAL MARKET REPORT
Forbes
STEVE FORBES
How Capitalism Will Save Us

May 23, 2005
"It's Cellevision: Entertainment Is Lighting Up Your Phone"

July 24, 2006
"Vladimir Putin: Russia's Energy Tsar"

September 5, 2005
Forbes Asia debuts

February 12, 2007
"Rupert 2.0: How Murdoch Creates Tomorrow's News"

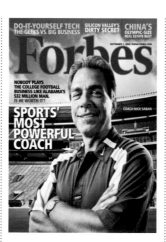

September 1, 2008
"Nick Saban: Sports' Most Powerful Coach"

December 28, 2009
"Google Wants to Own Your Mind"

2005　　**2006**　　**2007**　　**2008**　　**2009**

2010s

PIRATES BEWARE: JANUARY 16, 2012

THE MOST IMPORTANT MAN in music over the past decade is a laconic Swede named Daniel Ek, who achieved global renown (and an immense fortune) before his 30th birthday. He did so by offering blessed salvation to an industry badly beleaguered by the digital revolution: His streaming service, Spotify, would offer, he said, a platform "more enticing to consumers than piracy while . . . providing a sustainable revenue model." That was the grail musicians and executives alike had sought, mostly in vain, since Napster upended its entire business model more than ten years prior.

Forbes trained a spotlight on Ek well before Spotify became as ubiquitous as compact discs and cassettes once were. "I should be home in bed," he lamented to us, having just returned to Stockholm and yet already planning another trip to New York for his first-ever press conference. "But we need to get this thing perfect."

Today Spotify has more than 60 million subscribers in over 60 countries who pay around $10 a month for a growing catalog of some 30 million songs. In a way, though, Ek is a prominent face of something far bigger—a technological transformation that *Forbes*' newest franchise, 30 Under 30, catalogs all year long. (Fittingly, the list debuted in the issue fronted by Ek.) As *Forbes* editor Randall Lane would later write, young entrepreneurs are "no longer content merely conquering the technology space—every industry is now the technology space, whether hotels or music or transportation. And thus ripe for pillaging."

December 20, 2010
"Julian Assange Wants to Spill Your Corporate Secrets"

September 12, 2011
"Christine Lagarde Takes Control"

June 4, 2012:
"Celebrity 100, Justin Bieber"

February 11, 2013
"Airbnb's Brian Chesky: Turning Homes Into Hotels"

December 15, 2014
"Philanthropy: The Visionaries Reimagining Our Children's Future"

| 2010 | 2011 | 2012 | 2013 | 2014 |

HEROES OF PHILANTHROPY: OCTOBER 8, 2012

WHAT DOES $126 BILLION look like? After looking at this cover image—likely the greatest wealth ever captured in a single portrait—you now know.

On June 26, 2012, 161 billionaires and near-billionaires came together in New York for *Forbes'* inaugural Summit on Philanthropy, a chance for the most successful people on the planet to use their resources (and the minds that built all that success) to try to solve the world's most intractable problems.

Toward the end of the day, a dozen of the world's top philanthropists gathered in one room. No digital wizardry; they were all in one place at one time. The entire shoot took just 15 minutes, thanks to weeks of prep work by the photo crew—testing cameras, the room, the lights. The cover was shot dozens of times in advance using stand ins to ensure perfect illumination and focus when the actual subjects arrived.

When they did, it was magic. Warren Buffett, Oprah Winfrey, Bill Gates, Melinda French Gates, Pete Peterson, Leon Black, Jon Bon Jovi, Marc Benioff, David Rubenstein, Steve Case, Laura Arrillaga-Andreessen and Marc Andreessen: $126 billion of personal net worth, extraordinary business achievement—and a desire to change the world on an enormous scale.

October 19, 2015
"Donald Trump: 'I look better if I'm worth $10 billion than $4 billion.'"

August 23, 2016
"Instagram: The $50 Billion Grand Slam That's Driving Facebook's Future."

july 27, 2017
"Bitcoin Spawns $100 Billion Cryptocurrency Mania"

2015　　　2016　　　2017

FORBES EVOLVES

On May 12, 1997, a new website, ingloriously named the "Forbes Digital Tool," blinked to life. The first edition featured columns by luminaries such as Katharine Graham, the celebrity publisher of the *Washington Post,* bond salesman turned best-selling author Po Bronson and humorist Christopher Buckley, who pointedly titled his contribution "Is Anyone Out There?" In the era of painfully slow dialup modems, AOL accounts and bumbling pre-Google search engines, that was an excellent question.

Initially, the answer was a resounding "no." The site's tiny, inexperienced staff struggled to publish three or four stories a day, each a laboriously crafted HTML page, into verticals including "tech," "new media," "personal finance" and a lifestyle section called (really) "Digital Cool." But when, in the spring of 1998, a young reporter named Adam Penenberg uncovered the unthinkable fabrications of Stephen Glass at the *New Republic,* creating global news (and eventually the movie *Shattered Glass*), Forbes.com was firmly on the nation's radar.

Exponential growth has followed, much of it the result of Lewis D'Vorkin's return in 2010. D'Vorkin had been a top editor at the magazine in the 1990s, before a gig at AOL and a turn as an internet entrepreneur. Seemingly overnight, everyone on staff had their own page on which to post stories, and thousands of outside contributors—with a focus on experts in their fields—gave the site sustainable scope and scale. Eventually, with BrandVoice, consumer companies, labeled transparently for readers, could post stories as well.

It worked. Forbes.com is now the world's largest in the business category, and Forbes' digital revenues dwarf those generated by print or any other part of the company. We now have a definitive answer to Buckley's question: *Everyone* is out there.

1997
Forbes.com launches, making it one of the first media websites.

2010
—
The introduction of an entirely new ad concept—
AdVoice, and our earliest partner SAP.

2016
Taking storytelling into new dimensions, with the evolution of
BrandVoice and a special feature page showcasing The Macallan.

2017
Built for speed and
consumption, anywhere.

ADVERTISING AND FORBES

Starting with our first issue—the then-groundbreaking National Cash Register Company sits on page one—advertising has always been an integral part of the *Forbes* experience. There were some years during the Malcolm Forbes era, and again in the 90's, when *Forbes* was running as many ads as any magazine in the world. Decade by decade, you can watch the free market and the consumer culture mature, glossy page after glossy page. These are a few of our favorites, including many from our best or longest-running partners.

1924
IBM

1932
MetLife

1957
Sheraton

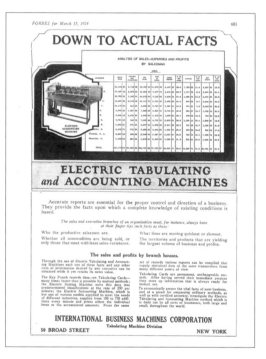

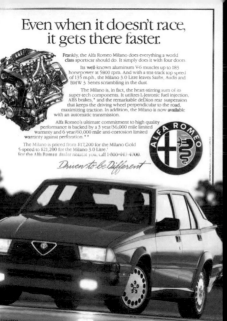

Even when it doesn't race, it gets there faster.

Frankly, the Alfa Romeo Milano does everything a world class sportscar should do. It simply does it with four doors.

Its well-known aluminum V-6 muscles up to 183 horsepower at 5800 rpm. And with a test-track top speed of 135 m.p.h., the Milano 3.0 Litre leaves Saabs, Audis and BMW 3 Series scrambling in the dust.

The Milano is, in fact, the heart-stirring sum of its super-tech components. It utilizes L-Jetronic fuel injection, ABS brakes,* and the remarkable deDion rear suspension that keeps the driving wheel perpendicular to the road, maximizing traction. In addition, the Milano is now available with an automatic transmission.

Alfa Romeo's ultimate commitment to high quality performance is backed by a 3 year/36,000 mile limited warranty and 6 year/60,000 mile anti-corrosion limited warranty against perforation.**

The Milano is priced from $17,200 for the Milano Gold 5-speed to $21,200 for the Milano 3.0 Litre.' For the Alfa Romeo dealer nearest you, call 1-800-447-4700.

Driven to be Different

ALFA ROMEO

Cartier

Tank® Française Watch
18K gold.
Steel and 18K gold.
Steel.

TWO WORLDS, ONE MACALLAN

DOUBLE CASK
12 YEARS OLD

Traditional sherry-seasoned casks from both sides of the Atlantic. Defined by a new, unmistakable American Oak style.

THE MACALLAN
12
DOUBLE CASK

The MACALLAN
HIGHLAND SINGLE MALT
SCOTCH WHISKY

100 GREATEST BUSINESS MINDS

While Forbes prides itself on quantifiable lists—the richest, the biggest, the highest—assembling the 100 greatest living business minds was inherently a subjective affair. More than a dozen editors met dozens of times over two years, debating membership criteria for a list that started more than three times this size. We looked for people who either created something with substantial impact on the world, or who innovated in their field in a manner with major ramifications outside it. The honorees you'll see here actively participated—all the essays and portraits are original. The collective result is a master class on business, a visual time capsule—and 100 lessons for the next 100 years.

SHELDON ADELSON

CLIMBER: FROM TRADE SHOWS (COMDEX) TO CASINOS (SANDS: LAS VEGAS, MACAU, SINGAPORE) TO POLITICAL POWER (GOP)

You don't always have to be the guy that comes up with a new idea from scratch. If you can **take an old concept, like vending or gambling, and just put a new spin on it, success will follow you like a shadow.**

When I was 16, I bought a bunch of vending machines. At the time, they were set up inside factories, which meant people only bought snacks during the 40-hour workweek. So I moved the machines into gas stations, where cab drivers were lining up 24 hours a day, seven days a week. Money came rolling in.

Years later I did a similar thing with casinos. Las Vegas had been successful in the United States, but China had a billion more people in it. Why not rebuild the Las Vegas Strip there? Everyone else in the gambling industry thought it was the dumbest idea ever. I charged ahead in Macau anyway. Now all the naysayers would cut off their right arm to get a piece of land there. I've got a warehouse full of right arms, and a couple of left ones, too.

PAUL ALLEN

SURVIVOR: COFOUNDER, MICROSOFT; INVESTOR AND PHILANTHROPIST (VULCAN); SPORTS TEAM OWNER; BRAIN SCIENCE BENEFACTOR

We are about to enter the era of deep medicine, where we understand cell pathways and how to change them. I'm a two-time cancer survivor. First I had Hodgkin's, a young person's cancer. And then non-Hodgkin's lymphoma. Right now they just hit you with everything they've got, like carpet bombing. And then my mother passed away of Alzheimer's.

Those things are motivating experiences that make you want to understand things better and then make a difference. In maybe 20 or 30 years, **we will use things like stem cells to change disease outcomes**—your own immune system, designed by evolution, to attack sick cells and things like that. It seems inconceivable now—we have thousands of types of cells, so there are trillions of combinations—but health care would be much more personal. And the costs would potentially decline.

43

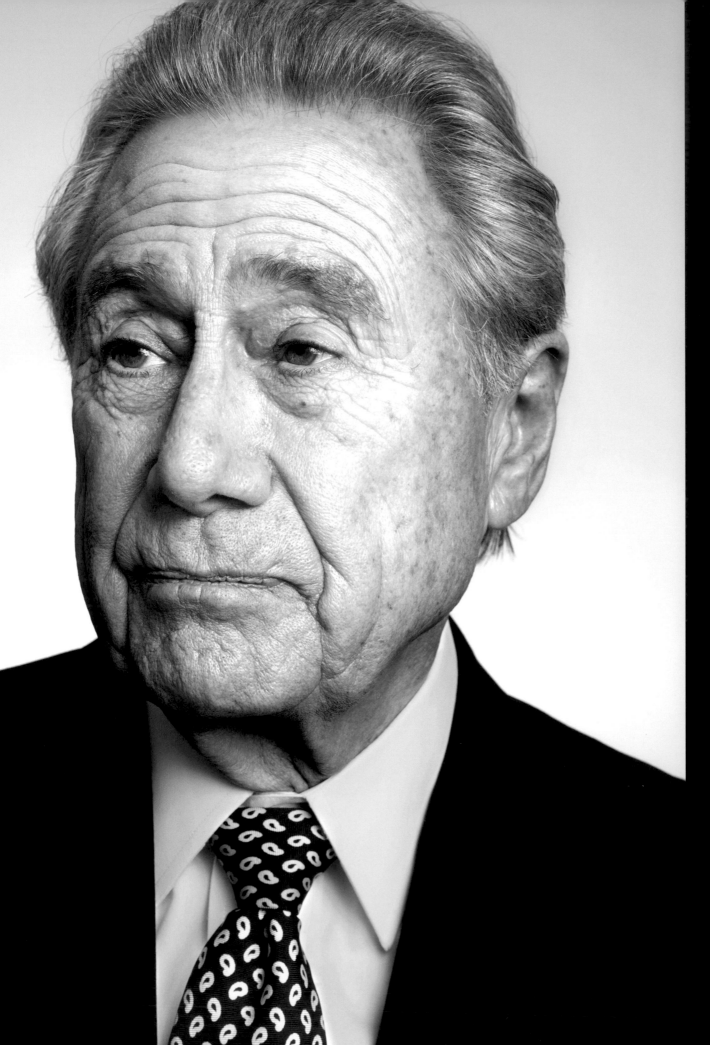

CONNECTOR: RAILROADS, QWEST, ENTERTAINMENT

I've always been intellectually curious. I like to **research how and why things are, and imagine how they might change.** Specifically, I look for industries in transition and try to anticipate opportunities that could arise from changes in underlying fundamentals. So far I've had decent timing when it comes to certain businesses, such as energy, railroads and telecom.

Deregulation changed the railroad and telephone industries. When I was running Southern Pacific, we realized that railroad rights-of-way were perfect paths to lay fiber-optic cables. So we started Qwest to lay important portions of the early backbone of the internet. I got a little nervous when Qwest had over $1 billion of fiber in the ground and no customers, but it wasn't long before we went from selling voice by the minute to selling data by the gigabyte.

With the rise of the digital world, I believed demand would grow for live analog entertainment like sports and music, so we started building and acquiring more than 100 unique venues, like the L.A. Staples Center and the O2 London, along with music, entertainment and teams to play in them like the Kings, Lakers and Galaxy. While the underlying concept was developing well-located real estate, the critical strategy was content.

A sector about to undergo transformational change is the power industry, driven in part by the rise of renewable clean energy, which has the potential to drive change, much like the advent of fiber optics drove change within the telephone business. I'm currently building what could be America's biggest wind farm.

Not everything of course always works as anticipated, but it helps to get into the habit of being curious and developing a willingness to accept the concept of risk.

GIORGIO ARMANI

STYLE ICON: FOUNDER, ARMANI

I always try to maintain a sense of reality and ensure that I surround myself with the right people, who understand the times in which we live. In this line of work, my team is crucial. **I'm the one who decides, but I like having lots of other people with whom I can discuss ideas,** as this helps with the creative process. In the world of fashion, five years is already a hundred, so going forward, the challenge will be to capture the attention of a public that is increasingly stimulated by countless offers and new forms of communication.

45

BERNARD ARNAULT

**ULTIMATE TASTEMAKER:
FOUNDER, LUXURY-GOODS
CONGLOMERATE LVMH**

The success of LVMH is built
on creativity, quality, entrepreneurship and, most importantly,
long-term vision. For instance, I
remember the first time I visited
China, in 1991. I arrived in Bei-
jing—I saw no cars, only bicycles,
no tall buildings. The GDP was 4%
of what it is today. Nonetheless,
we decided to open our first Louis
Vuitton store in China. Today
Louis Vuitton is the number one
luxury brand in the country and
across the world.

We have been seeing for the past
25 years a growing desire for high-
quality products and an accelera-
tion of buying power. Nowadays,
the internet makes the planet
much smaller. Product launches
now need to be global in order
to be successful. **When you start
something today, you usually
have to start it all over the world
at the same time** to be successful,
and you can see what's going on
anywhere, instantly. That requires
higher investment—which gives us
an advantage. Creating increasingly desirable new products and
selling them worldwide is what
LVMH does best.

BILLY BEANE

THE MONEYBALL MAN: OAKLAND A'S EXECUTIVE VICE PRESIDENT

In sports, you're not allowed to just survive. People cheer for teams that win. And it's a zero-sum game. You don't get partial credit for losing. I never doubted the Moneyball approach. We had two choices—intuition or data. Before, it seemed like we were making decisions on a roulette wheel, and when we were correct we celebrated the good guesses and applied some sort of clairvoyance to it, as opposed to just pure luck and random outcome.

So instead, we were very rational, logical and fact-based. What was interesting was the resistance. When we applied data to decision making and relied on objective reasoning, it was held to a perfect standard. If it was not correct 100% of the time, the response was "I told you that number shit doesn't work." But it did work. And then we had to evolve again. As soon as you think you've completely figured it out, you're probably in trouble. **Every business is a living document, an algorithm that needs to be improved.**

MARC BENIOFF

ORACLE ESCAPEE: FOUNDER, SALESFORCE

We are living in the fourth industrial revolution, with advancements in robotics, genetics, stem cells, autonomous vehicles and especially artificial intelligence. All will dramatically change life itself. **We need to have a beginner's mind to think about what is happening.** That idea of the beginner's mind is the core to innovation. When you ask, What do you want and what do you dream, you're able to ask yourself, What am I beginning? People who lose their relevance get stuck in the past because they're no longer in the present moment.

TIM BERNERS-LEE
VISIONARY: INVENTOR, WORLD WIDE WEB

I published my proposal for the World Wide Web in 1989. From the outset, I imagined it as an open, universal space, where anyone, anywhere could take their ideas and bring them to life without having to ask for permission or pay royalties. I hardwired these factors into the Web's design and made a conscious decision not to try to copyright or patent it. In 1993, CERN, my employers at the time, agreed to make the code available to anyone, royalty-free, forever.

This openness is at the core of what makes the Web powerful. It has underpinned the decades of creativity and innovation, opening up access to information, letting us communicate and collaborate across borders, and creating new industries. But now, as the Web matures, this openness is under threat.

Some governments have stepped up censorship of information they feel threatened by, using Web-based technologies to monitor citizens or even shutting down the internet in their jurisdiction. And some companies are also trying to limit openness for financial gain by challenging the principle that all internet traffic is treated equally—net neutrality. The internet is both a market for bandwidth and a market enabler (content, social networks, etc.). Strong net neutrality rules separating these markets are key. Otherwise, one set of interests can control the other—a disaster for innovation.

The open Web has been fertile ground for entrepreneurs to build successful companies—without having to ask permission from internet providers to allow their idea to take off. You break that "permissionless" space, and you establish substantial barriers for the Web's next big thing.

The open Web, like all open markets, demands rules to ensure it stays fair and competitive. **For the economic, social and political benefit of all, the Web must be recognized as a public good** and locked open through appropriate corporate and government action—including the preservation of net neutrality. No single individual can control the future of the Web, but together we can keep it open and build the Web we want.

JEFF BEZOS

THE SAM WALTON OF THE 21ST CENTURY: FOUNDER, AMAZON

We're in the midst of a gigantic transition, where customers have incredible power as a result of transparency and word of mouth. It used to be that if you made a customer happy, they would tell five friends. Now with the megaphone of the internet, whether online customer reviews or social media, they can tell 5,000 friends. In the old days, an inferior product could prevail in the marketplace with superior marketing. Today customers can tell whether product and service is good because there's so much transparency. They can compare it to others very easily, and then they can tell all their friends—the **customers will do part of the heavy lifting, marketing-wise.** Rather than inferior products shouting louder, we have sort of a product meritocracy. It's very good for customers, it's very good for the companies that embrace it—and it's very good for society.

50

SARA BLAKELY

**RAGS TO (BILLION-DOLLAR)
RICHES: FOUNDER, CEO, SPANX**

In the early days of Spanx, I didn't vet
the manufacturer helping me make
our first product, footless pantyhose.
They went out of business and gave
me one week's notice. It almost put
Spanx under. Had I done any kind
of financial due diligence on them, I
would have been able to prevent that.
**Early-stage entrepreneurs shouldn't
forget about that layer.** It almost
stopped everything for me.

ARTHUR BLANK

BUILDER: COFOUNDER, HOME DEPOT; OWNER, ATLANTA FALCONS

When I was running Home Depot, I'd always stop the customers who walked out of our stores with nothing. They were the ones who taught us the most. Odds were, they didn't come to Home Depot just to walk around. They came because they wanted to buy something. And somehow, we had let them down. Wrong stuff, wrong price, bad service—something. They would tell us what the issue was, and then we would go in and fix the problem.

I took the same approach after buying the Atlanta Falcons. At the time, 40% of our stadium was empty. Our players needed a full house of our fans, but half of the people who came to games were rooting for the other team. So I went around the city asking people why they weren't buying tickets. I didn't ask Falcons employees—they had been trying to get people into the stadium since 1966, and they hadn't figured it out yet. I asked everyone else I met. Why don't you come to the Georgia Dome? They always had some explanation. We made a list of the problems and then fixed them. This is my 15th year as an owner, and we've sold out every game except for two.

Business isn't all that complicated. **If someone is out in the desert walking around, they're going to be thirsty. You just have to ask them what they want to drink.** If you have the humility to listen to other people rather than just hawking stuff, you're going to have a lot of customers. Too many businesspeople have big egos and aren't willing to ask.

MICHAEL BLOOMBERG

DOER: FINTECH AND MEDIA PIONEER; SOLUTIONS-ORIENTED MAYOR; PHILANTHROPIST

I was fired from Salomon Brothers in 1981 in part because no one at the firm thought much of my idea for computerizing financial data and analysis and presenting it in real time. Back then, most financial professionals didn't know how to use a computer, much less have one on their desk.

Organizations resist innovation—and those that do inevitably fail—because **people are more comfortable with what they know than with what they don't.** Looking beyond the horizon and taking risks have always been a core part of our company's culture, which we brought to New York's city hall and worked hard to spread throughout city government.

In both the public and private sectors, innovation requires hiring smart, creative and driven people, empowering them to take risks and standing behind them—in a public way—when things don't go as hoped. The biggest management failures in both business and government are not missed targets but missed opportunities.

JACK BOGLE

INDEX FUND POPULARIZER: FOUNDER, VANGUARD, WORLD'S LARGEST MUTUAL FUND COMPANY

In 1965, my mentor, Walter L. Morgan, the founder of Wellington Management Co., called me into his office. It was the go-go era, and we only had a conventional, balanced mutual fund. "I want you to do whatever it takes to fix the company. You're in charge now." I was 35. So I merged with a very aggressive equity fund out of Boston with managers younger than I was. **It seemed like an act of genius, until it wasn't.** The go-go era fell apart, and they turned out to be terrible money managers. In January 1974, the board of Wellington Management, controlled by that Boston group, fired me.

Except that the mutual funds themselves had a separate board controlled by independent directors, and I persuaded that board not to fire me. So there was a big fight, and it was resolved with a terrible deal: I would continue as chairman and CEO of the funds, which would be responsible for their own legal, compliance, administration and record keeping. (And I had to come up with a new name—that was the start of Vanguard Group.) My rivals, the people who fired me, would continue to oversee distribution, marketing and investment management. The scheme was totally irrational.

I had to find a way for Vanguard to take on the investment management and distribution of our funds. I had done some work on index funds in my senior thesis at Princeton in 1951. I had experienced the failure of active management firsthand. And I had just read an article by Nobel Laureate Paul Samuelson, saying, in essence, "Somebody, somewhere, please start an index fund." I took the idea to the board and they said "You can't get into investment management," and I said, "This fund has no investment management." They bought it, and there's where the index revolution began.

Then I decided we couldn't allow Wellington and its sales force to continue to distribute the funds—so we eliminated all sales commissions and went no-load overnight. The directors said "You're not allowed to take over distribution," and I said "We're not taking it over; we're eliminating it." They bought it, again.

When a door closes, if you look long enough and hard enough, if you're strong enough, you'll find a window that opens.

54

BONO

PURPOSE-DRIVEN ROCK STAR: LEAD SINGER, U2; COFOUNDER, ONE, (RED), ELEVATION PARTNERS, RISE FUND

Capitalism is not immoral, but it is amoral. And it requires our instruction. It's a wild beast that needs to be tamed, a better servant than master.

That's my philosophy with (RED), which partners with corporations to direct profits to fighting HIV/AIDS. The idea really came about after meeting with former Treasury secretary Bob Rubin, where he said, "You have to tell Americans the scale of the problem and what they can do about it. And you have to go about that like Nike does: They spend $50 million on ad campaigns." And I said, "Well, where are we going to get that kind of money?" And he said, "You're clever. You'll figure it out."

And we did. I realized that going to big companies and trying to break into their more modest philanthropy funds was a huge missed opportunity. It was their robust marketing and publicity budgets that we needed. Think of the creative minds in those departments— the messaging is the most important thing in keeping an issue "hot," making it relevant. Fighting HIV is very difficult. Activists often demonize the corporate world. It's easy to do, but **I think it's just foolishness to not recognize the creativity that you can unlock in the corporate world,** together with the entertainment world. (RED) has so far generated nearly $500 million for the fight against AIDS, but the heat (RED) companies have created has also helped pressure governments to do their part—and that's where the big money is, with donor governments spending $87.5 billion on HIV/AIDS since 2002. That's the reason we all do this!

Some of the most selfish people I've met are artists— I'm one of them—and some of the most selfless people I've ever met are in business, people like Warren Buffett. So, I've never had that clichéd view of commerce and culture being different. I always remember Björk saying to me that her songs, she feels, are like carpentry. Like her friends in Iceland, one of them designs a chair. Is that more beautiful or useful than a song? Well, it depends on the chair. Or the song. I've always seen what I do as an activist, as an artist, as an investor, as coming from the same place.

Great melodies have a lot in common with great ideas. They're instantly memorable. There's a certain inevitability. There's a sort of beautiful arc. Whether it's a song or business or a solution to a problem facing the world's poor, I see what I do as the same thing. I look for the topline melody, a clear thought. Now, my friends—and sometimes my bandmates and sometimes my family—would see this as multiple personality disorder. But for me, it's all the same thing.

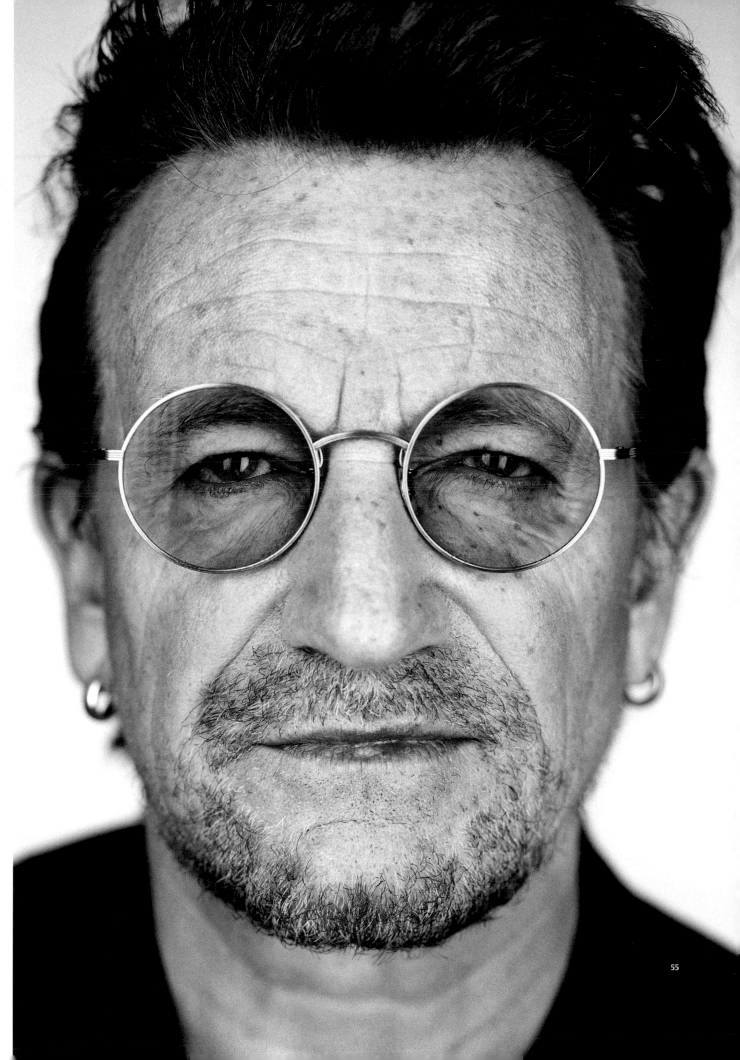

RICHARD BRANSON

THRILLIONAIRE: CONSUMMATE ENTREPRENEUR; FOUNDER, VIRGIN GROUP

I suppose that out of all the business-people in this issue, I've done a few more mad, zany things to get my companies on the map. Sometimes these stunts work, sometimes they don't. When Virgin America launched its Las Vegas route, my staff took me to the top of the Palms Hotel there and told me that I had to jump off the top floor into the party on the bottom floor on a bungee. I was very skeptical—the wind was blowing 50 miles an hour. **But I jumped and hit the side of the building on the way down, completely ripping my trousers off.** Blood poured down my legs as I arrived to the party. The Virgin brand is quite intricately linked with me personally, so I have to be careful not to go and damage the brand myself.

But that doesn't mean not taking risks. As the Virgin Group has gotten much bigger and much stronger, we can afford to take bigger, bolder risks in lots and lots of different sectors. One of our biggest investments has been the space companies, which we have already invested $1 billion to set up. We take tons of risks in life, whether personal risks or business risks. We sometimes fall flat on our face. But people don't mind people who try things and fail.

ELI BROAD

**SERIAL ENTREPRENEUR
(KB HOME, SUNAMERICA);
MAJOR PHILANTHROPIST**

If you look at all the companies in the new economy, whether it's Amazon, Uber, Facebook or Google, reasonable people wouldn't have done that. George Bernard Shaw said the reasonable man adapts himself to the world, the unreasonable person doesn't; therefore all progress comes from unreasonable people. I think my wife gave me a plaque that said that shortly after we were married. Being unreasonable allowed me to do things: Leaving the profession of accounting to start a homebuilding company; to take a traditional life insurance company and change it into a retirement-savings company, which we then sold to AIG for $18 billion, which then allowed me to become a full-time philanthropist.

I think the best thing to do is follow the advice that reasonable people maintain the status quo—those who are unreasonable make changes. **I have yet to meet a scientist who wants to maintain the status quo.** I hope philanthropists will do things that government can't or won't do. If you're a government bureaucrat, if you make a mistake, you're going to be out. A lot of things that have started with philanthropy then became of interest to government. In philanthropy we don't worry about getting fired. There's a lot of work to be done.

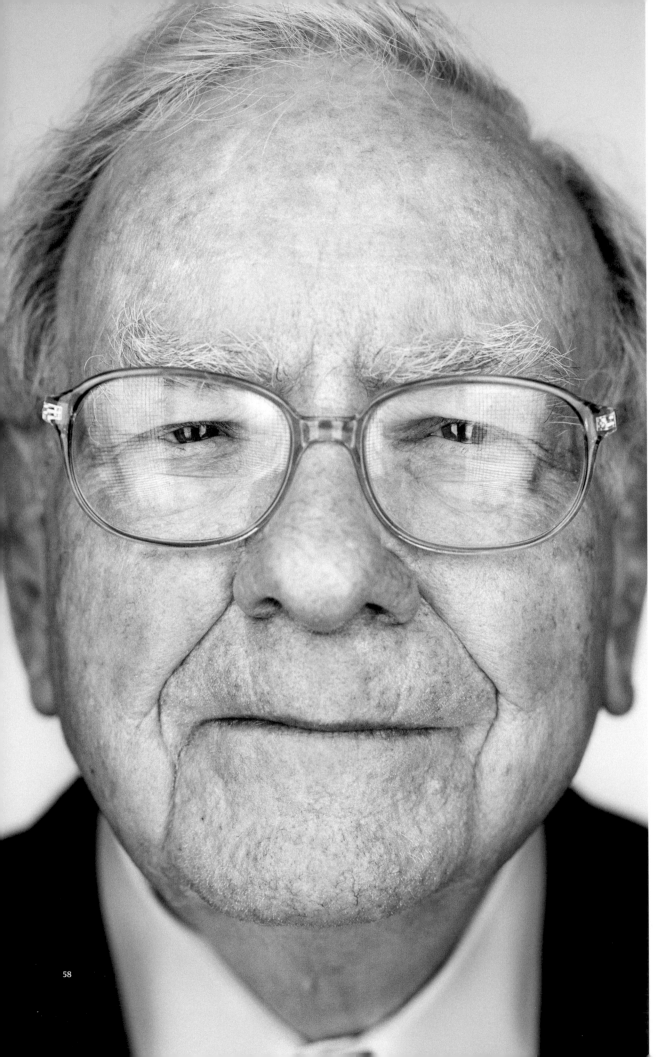

WARREN BUFFETT

THE ORACLE: CEO, BERKSHIRE HATHAWAY; ARGUABLY THE GREATEST INVESTOR AND BIGGEST PHILANTHROPIST OF ALL TIME

When I was 7 or 8 years old, I was lucky in that I found a subject that really interested me—investing. I read every book on that topic in the Omaha Public Library by the time I was 11. Some of them more than once. My dad happened to be in the investment business, so when I would go down to have lunch with him on Saturdays, or whenever it might be, I would pick up the books around his office and start reading. (If he'd been a shoe salesman, I might be a shoe salesman now.)

I bought the book that became the largest influence on my investing life by accident, while I was at the University of Nebraska. I read and reread *The Intelligent Investor*, by Benjamin Graham, about half a dozen times—it's incredibly sound philosophy, very well written and easy to understand. And it gave me an investment philosophy that I'm still using today.

That strategy is to **find a good business—and one that I can understand why it's good—with a durable, competitive advantage, run by able and honest people, and available at a price that makes sense.** Because we're not going to sell the business, we don't need something with earnings that go up the next month or the next quarter; we need something that will earn more money 10 and 20 and 30 years from now. And then we want a management team we admire and trust.

My favorite investment, one that embodies this philosophy, is Geico, which I learned about when I was 20 years old, because I got on a train and went down to Washington and banged on the door on a Saturday until Lorimer Davidson, who would later become CEO, responded. He answered my questions, taught me the insurance business and explained to me the competitive advantage that Geico had. That afternoon changed my life.

Here's a product that now costs, on average, about $1,800 a year. People don't want to buy it—but they do want to drive. And they hope they never use it, because they don't want to have an accident. And Geico was a way to deliver that product for less money than people had been paying. When Berkshire bought control of it in 1995, it had about a 2% market share; now it has a 12% market share, and we are saving the American public perhaps $4 billion a year against what they would be paying if they had bought insurance the way they had before. A simple idea when Leo Goodwin founded the company in 1936. The same simple idea now.

Ben Franklin said it a long time ago: "Keep thy shop and thy shop will keep thee." The quaint language aside, it means don't just satisfy your customers—delight them. They're gonna talk to other people. They're going to come back. Anybody who has happy customers is likely to have a pretty good future.

But ultimately, there's one investment that supersedes all others: Invest in yourself. Address whatever you feel your weaknesses are, and do it now. I was terrified of public speaking when I was young. I couldn't do it. It cost me $100 to take a Dale Carnegie course, and it changed my life. I got so confident about my new ability, I proposed to my wife during the middle of the course. It also helped me sell stocks in Omaha, despite being 21 and looking even younger. Nobody can take away what you've got in yourself—and everybody has potential they haven't used yet. If you can increase your potential 10%, 20% or 30% by enhancing your talents, they can't tax it away. Inflation can't take it from you. You have it the rest of your life.

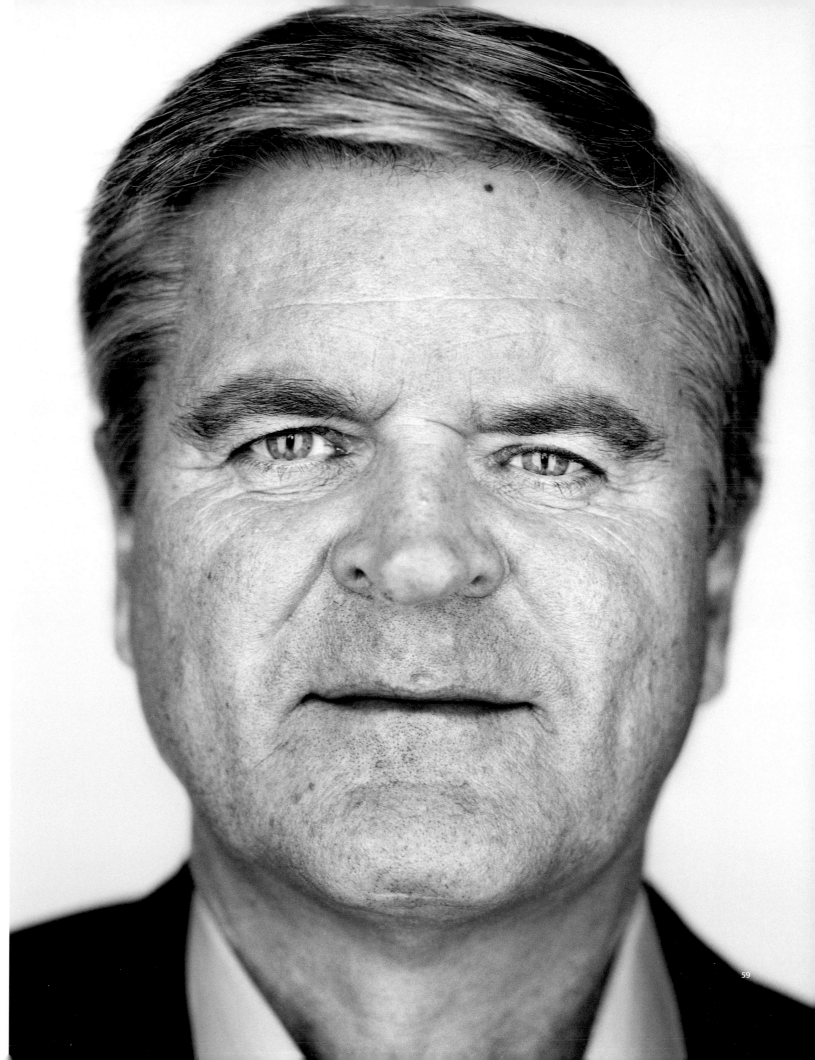

STEVE CASE

INTERNET ENABLER: COFOUNDER, AOL; VENTURE CAPITAL DISPERSER: COFOUNDER, REVOLUTION

The story of American business over the last 100 years is a story about different sectors rising and falling (and often rising again, in unanticipated ways) in different regions of the country. When Detroit was an automobile powerhouse and Pittsburgh was the steel city, Silicon Valley was just fruit orchards. As the industrial revolution peaked and the technology revolution accelerated, the role of those places changed.

Today 75% of venture capital still goes to three states (California, New York and Massachusetts); half goes to California alone. As we enter the internet's third wave, where entrepreneurs will leverage technology to disrupt major real-world sectors—like health care, education, financial services—startups will increasingly move to cities where industry expertise exists. The opportunity to grow companies that spur job creation and economic growth holds great promise for I what I call these "Rise of the Rest" cities. This will lead to **a more dispersed innovating economy, where jobs and wealth are created all across the country,** not just on the coasts. We need to level the playing field so that everyone, everywhere, has a shot at the American dream.

MORRIS CHANG

COMPUTER INSIDER: FOUNDER TAIWAN SEMICONDUCTOR

My values are: integrity, commitment, innovation and trust from customers. Integrity means honesty and **willingness to fulfill a promise,** even at high cost. Commitment means dedication and loyalty to a task or an organization. Innovation means change. Trust from customers of course has to be earned, and I try to earn it by integrity and commitment.

DHANIN CHEARAVANONT

AMALGAMATOR: SENIOR CHAIRMAN, CP GROUP

Each industrial age is different. We are now in an era when the younger generation is redefining the market with startups, technology and innovation. In this new world, everything happens and changes very quickly. Successful people today are both innovators and disruptors— they create something that was not there before. Most importantly, we need to appreciate that the success we have today can be taken away tomorrow and that there are more capable people with better technology that we need to keep up with. If we are complacent and not open to change, we will soon lose our place.

The best way to stay ahead is to learn from the younger generation. The knowledge and thought processes among people who grew up in Industry 3.0, when computers were new concepts, compared to Industry 4.0, when robots and AI are revolutionizing production processes, are very different. The new generation will always lead us to new innovations and ways of doing things we could never have imagined before.

61

BRIAN CHESKY

**HOTEL DISRUPTOR,
SHARING-ECONOMY POINT PERSON:
COFOUNDER, AIRBNB**

Pablo Picasso once said, "It took me four years to paint like Raphael, but a lifetime to paint like a child." I think you must always live and think like a child. Or have that childlike curiosity and wonder. That's probably the most important trait you can have, especially as an entrepreneur. And even though I'm still young, I try to always look at what people significantly younger than me are doing. What's the next thing? **I like to imagine the world five years from now. Or imagine what I want the world to look like five years from now.** And when I think back to when we started Airbnb, we were trying to challenge the status quo. Now we're trying to challenge ourselves.

JIM COLLINS

CONSULTANT, AUTHOR: *GOOD TO GREAT* **AND** *BUILT TO LAST*

Peter Drucker made the biggest impact upon me in a personal moment when he hit me with a challenge, like a Zen master thwacking the table with a bamboo stick to get the attention of a wayward student. "It seems to me you spend a lot of time worrying about how you will survive," he said in his resonant Austrian accent, referring to my anxiety in leaving my comfortable faculty teaching post at Stanford to carve a self-directed intellectual path at age 36. "**And you seem to spend a lot of energy on the question of how to be successful. But that is the wrong question!**" Then, pausing for effect, "The question is, how to be *useful.*"

63

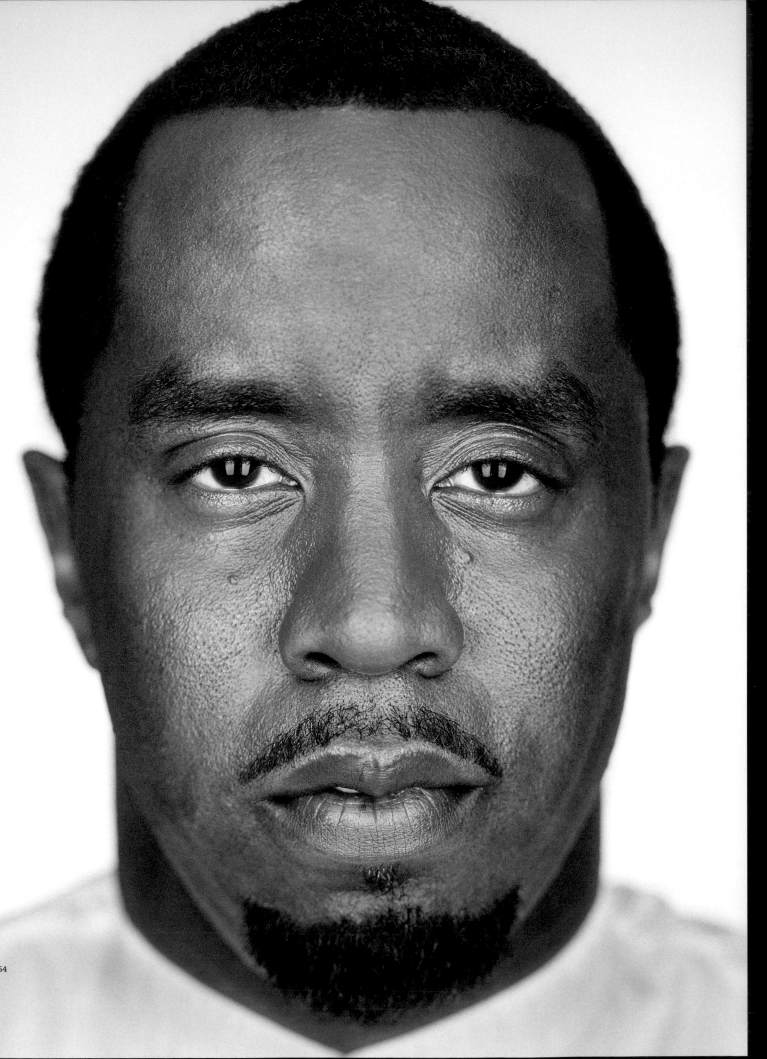

64

SEAN "DIDDY" COMBS

HIP-HOP MOGUL (BAD BOY); FASHION MOGUL (SEAN JOHN); LIQUOR MOGUL (CÎROC)

I started my business career at age 12, delivering newspapers. I had a lot of elderly customers, so I would always put the newspaper in between the screen door and the door—**that caring made me different, made me better** than the last paperboy. Since then, I've always understood that if I give the customers my best, and serviced them differently, whether music, clothing or vodka, I'll get a return on my hard work.

RAY DALIO

KING OF THE HEDGE FUND MANAGERS: FOUNDER, BRIDGEWATER ASSOCIATES (WORLD'S LARGEST HEDGE FUND)

I think that the most important issue that will reshape our lives in the years ahead will be how man-made and artificial intelligence compete and work together.

My views have been colored by experiences with algorithmic decision-making over the last 30 years, which have been fabulous. But it's a two-edged sword. I have learned that by thinking through my criteria for making decisions, writing them down as principles and then expressing them as algorithms so that the computer thinks in parallel with me, **I can make much better decisions than I could make alone.** It has also helped us to have an idea meritocracy that produces collective decision-making that's much better than individual decision-making. But our path to doing this was to work with the computer to gain deep understanding.

JOHN PAUL DEJORIA

SELF-MADE BILLIONAIRE—TWICE: COFOUNDER, JOHN PAUL MITCHELL SYSTEMS; COFOUNDER, PATRÓN TEQUILA

There's turnover of staff and then there's efficiency of staff. Companies sometimes hire ten people to do the job of three. What's the answer to it all? It's a basic thing that goes back to the law to do unto others as you would have others do unto you. **Treat and pay your staff exactly the way you'd want to be treated** if you were in their place.

Now, how does this work? John Paul Mitchell Systems is in almost 100 countries. We've been around for 37 years. My turnover is less than 100 people. Only two people have even retired from our company. They don't want to. They're having such a good time.

Someone once asked Francisco Alcaraz, the genius distiller creating all of our formulas for Patrón, "What is the secret? Why is Patrón so good? Why do people keep coming back?" He says, "The secret's very easy. It's called love. We are all treated so well, we love what we're doing. We never want to leave. We want every bottle to be reflective of us."

With Patrón, 53 people touch every single bottle; that's a lot of hands-on work, and they're all loved. If you work for me during the day shift, you get a free lunch by chefs. If you work for me at night during the night shift, you get a free lunch and dinner by chefs. You want to pray during the day? We built a chapel right in the middle of the 17th-century Spanish-French hacienda.

In all the businesses we're involved in it's the exact same way. If you love your people and let them know you're giving back, not just hoarding all the money for yourself, they want to join in.

LEONARDO DEL VECCHIO

VISION VISIONARY: FOUNDER, LUXOTTICA

One thing that hasn't changed in my years of doing business—I'm always doing and saying what I really think, acting with clarity and transparency. **I prefer to match words with deeds or let the facts speak for me.** I try to be what I really am and not what people would like me to be. There is a certain peace that comes with that. My reputation is truly my own.

MICHAEL DELL

**DORM-ROOM LEGEND:
FOUNDER, DELL TECHNOLOGIES**

The Computer Age is just beginning. Most companies today have about a thousand times more data than they actually use to make better decisions. When you overlay the latest in computer science—AI, machine learning, deep learning, unsupervised learning—you will create an explosion of opportunity and also a real emergency. Over the next few years, as the cost of making something intelligent approaches zero, **companies will succeed and fail based on their ability to translate data, including historical data, into insights and actions and products and services** in real time. We like to think of ourselves as a company with big ears: We listen, we learn, we understand—and we create things.

BARRY DILLER

MEDIA MOGUL: BOSS AT ABC, PARAMOUNT, 20TH CENTURY FOX; FOUNDER, IAC

Don't think of a specific job, so to speak, or a specific career, like "I'd like to be this" or "I'd like to be that." You should find an area that interests you and **just get on the highway, and it will lead you wherever you lead it.** For me, I've only really worked for three companies: ABC was eight years, Paramount was ten years, and Fox was eight years. That's my entire working-in-a-company life, so to speak. I got to a point where I wanted to work for myself. If you can, do it—which is more than just the word "can"; there's a lot cooked up in there—you should. You can control your own destiny, whatever that is, good or bad.

69

JOHN DOERR

VENTURE CAPITAL MIDAS

Here's how I stay relevant: **I read. I listen. I try to surround myself with smart people of all ages and backgrounds.** Most Wednesday nights, my wife, Ann, and I host a group of college students for dinner to share their worldviews and the work they are doing. They inspire me with their potential and passion to change the world.

JACK DORSEY

**MULTITASKING CEO:
TWITTER, SQUARE**

My biggest mistake was thinking
I shouldn't **show my mistakes**—I
learned I should.

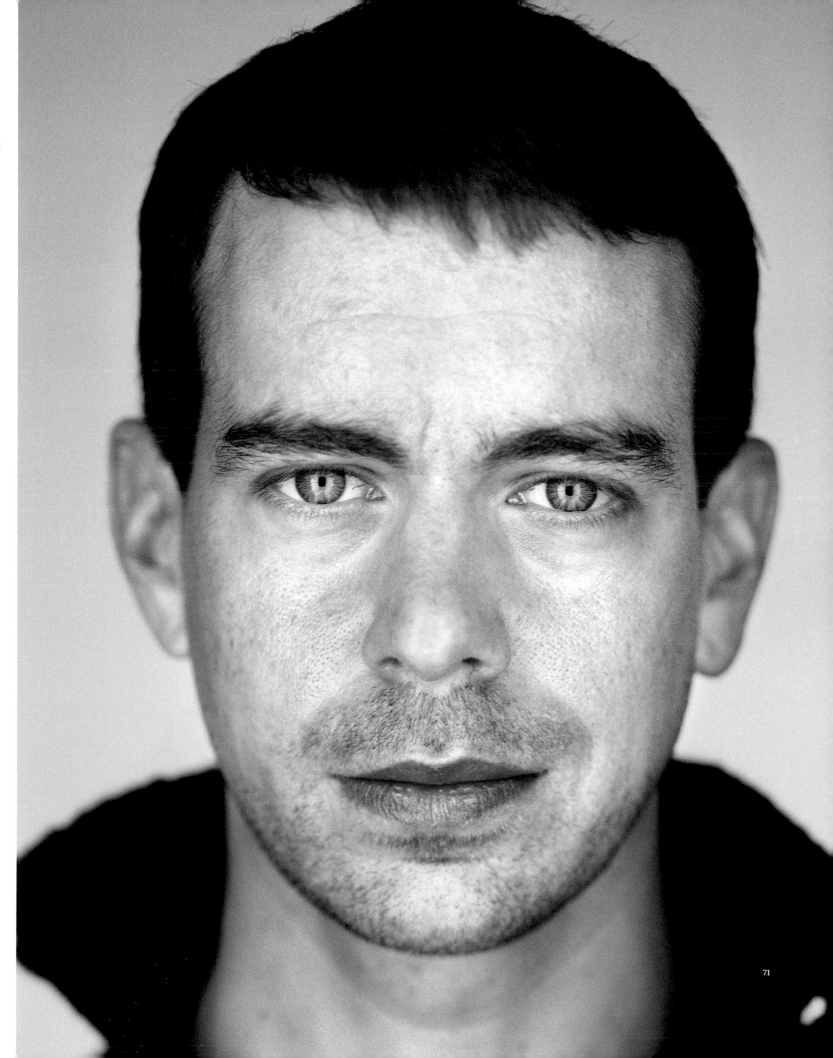

MICHAEL EISNER

**THE MOUSE THAT MIKE BUILT:
FORMER CEO, DISNEY**

In 1998, Disney bought Infoseek, then one of the largest search engines, behind Yahoo. Shortly thereafter, I was convinced in the men's room by a consultant at McKinsey that Infoseek shouldn't do advertised search because it wasn't the Disney way. I wasn't in my office, I wasn't thinking, and I said, "Oh, yeah. My job is to protect the Disney brand. We won't have advertised search, that's not clean." Google came around and did AdWords, and Infoseek didn't. It was probably a $200 billion mistake. After that, **we made a rule: No more meetings in the bathroom.**

LARRY GAGOSIAN

THE PICASSO OF ART DEALERS

There was a painting that Si Newhouse wanted to buy in the early 1980s—"Aloha" by Roy Lichtenstein. I had sold several paintings from that collection to him, and this Lichtenstein was $1 million. Only a handful of paintings had sold for $1 million at that time. So I said, "Let's write them a check." And Si, who is a billionaire, said, "No, I'm not going to write a check for $1 million. Let's pay them $100,000 a month." And when I asked him why, he said, **"I don't want them to think that money comes that easily."** If he were willing to write a check right away, he explained, it would influence the negotiation. It was a shrewd lesson, especially since "Aloha" would later become worth well over $100 million.

73

BILL GATES

TECH TITAN (COFOUNDER, MICROSOFT); GLOBAL PHILANTHROPIST (BILL & MELINDA GATES FOUNDATION); RICHEST PERSON IN THE WORLD (FOR NOW)

In early 1975, when I was in college, my friend Paul Allen showed me an issue of *Popular Electronics* featuring the Altair 8800 computer, the first commercially successful personal computer. We both had the same thought: "The revolution is going to happen without us!" We were sure that software was going to change the world, and **we worried that if we didn't join the digital revolution soon, it would pass us by.** That conversation marked the end of my college career and the beginning of Microsoft.

The next 100 years will create even more opportunities like that. Because it's so easy for someone with a great idea to share it with the world in an instant, the pace of innovation is accelerating—and that opens up more areas than ever for exploration. We've just begun to tap artificial intelligence's ability to help people be more productive and creative. The biosciences are filled with prospects for helping people live longer, healthier lives. Big advances in clean energy will make it more affordable and available, which will fight poverty and help us avoid the worst effects of climate change.

The potential for these advances is thrilling—they could save and improve the lives of millions—but they're not inevitable. They will happen only if people are willing to bet on a lot of crazy notions, knowing that while some won't work out, one breakthrough can change the world. Over the next 100 years, we need people to keep believing in the power of innovation and to take a risk on a few revolutionary ideas.

DAVID GEFFEN

ENTERTAINMENT ENTREPRENEUR: FOUNDER, ASYLUM RECORDS, GEFFEN RECORDS; COFOUNDER, DREAMWORKS

Being in business by yourself, you're responsible, one way or the other, and I had a lot of success that way. In 1994, Jeffrey Katzenberg, Steven Spielberg and I started DreamWorks. We had to borrow a billion dollars, and raise a billion dollars in equity, which created a huge responsibility for me. I never had any debt before that. I did it because I wanted to help Jeffrey, who had been fired at the Walt Disney Company. But it wasn't something I was passionate about. Partners have shared goals but also divergent ones. It was a commitment over 15 years, because **I wanted to stay until the investors got their money back.** That was very important to me. Starting a new studio was a thrilling challenge, but it was more stressful than fun. I never took a salary, a bonus or expenses. I learned never to do anything you're not passionate about. I gave all the money I earned from the $3.8 billion sale of the company to charity.

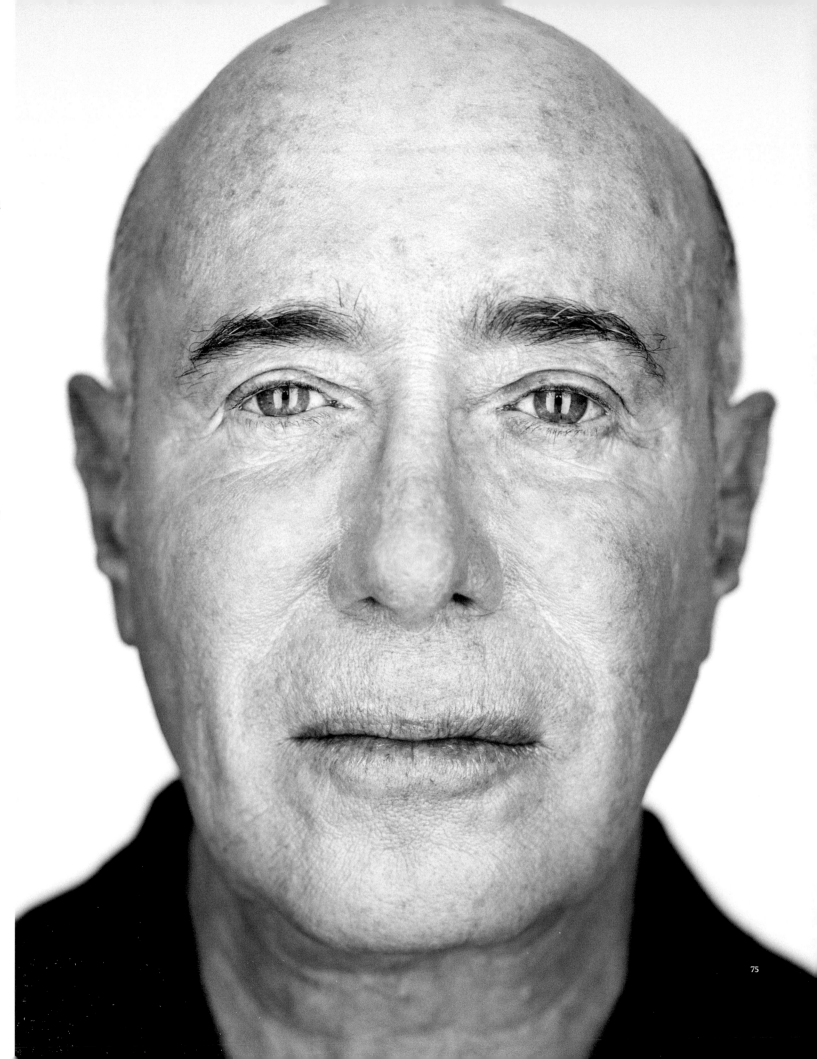

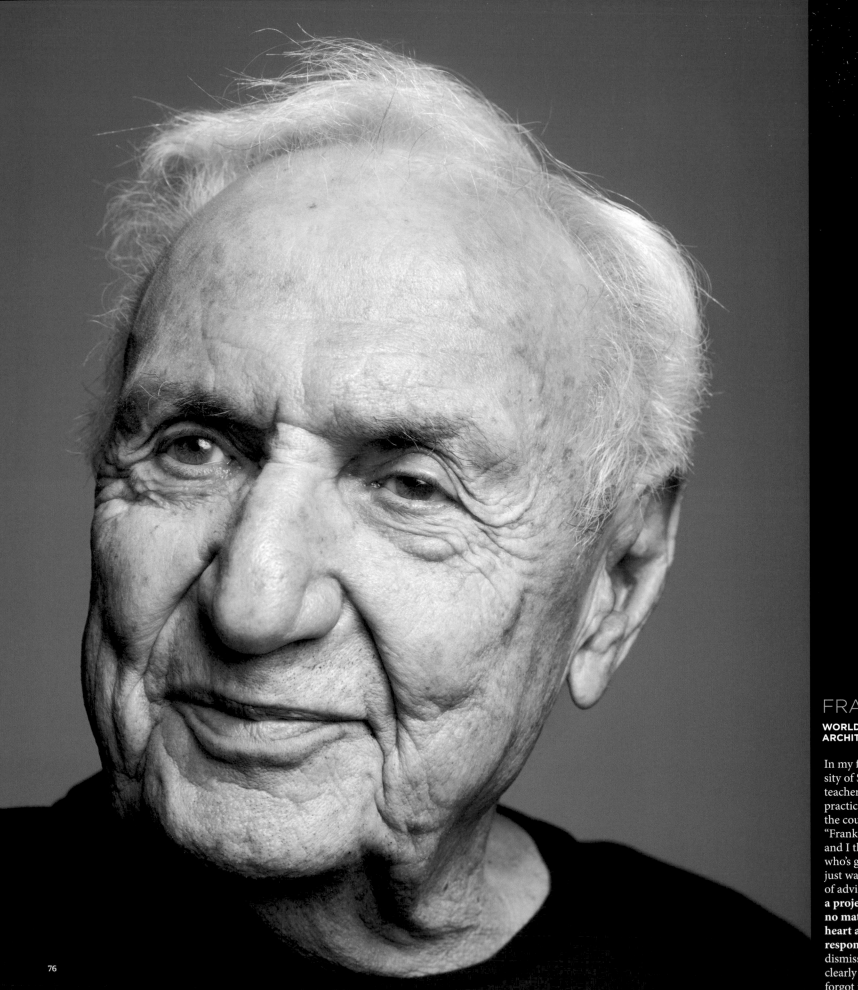

FRANK GEHRY

**WORLD-SHAPING
ARCHITECT**

In my fourth year at the University of Southern California, the teacher from my professional practice class came up to me in the courtyard one day and said, "Frank, I've been watching you, and I think you're a talented guy who's going to go somewhere. I just want to give you one word of advice: **No matter how small a project you work on, and no matter what it is, put your heart and soul and sense of responsibility into it**, and don't dismiss anything." He said it very clearly and lovingly, and I never forgot it and I've lived by it.

LOU GERSTNER

TURNAROUND SPECIALIST: FORMER CHAIRMAN AND CEO, IBM

When I arrived at IBM in 1993, I discovered that I had a number of businesses that were losing massive amounts of money, including one software product losing as much as $1 billion a year. I asked the question: What is the market share of this product? What are the customers saying? The answer: Our main competitor had 96% of the market; we had only 2%. But my technical people came back to me and said we had a better product, and my salespeople came back to me and said we had important customers that rely on this product.

I was early in my tenure, so I waited. But the fact was that the product was not being accepted by enough customers to be viable, and we eventually killed it. There are always reasons to go slow, many of them good ones. Yet, **when the decision is finally made, I've found my reaction is always the same: I should have done this a long time ago!**

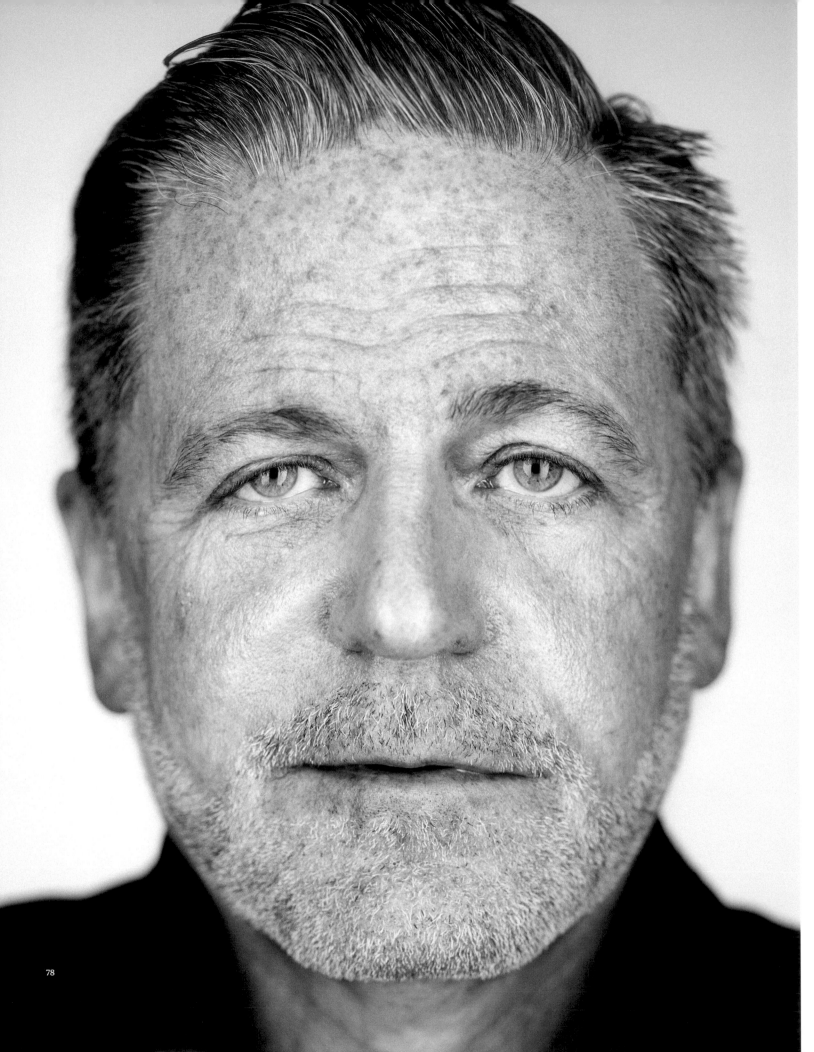

DAN GILBERT

BUILDER: FOUNDER, QUICKEN LOANS; OWNER, CLEVELAND CAVALIERS; DETROIT'S REVITALIZER

I have never seen anybody create a whole lot of wealth by chasing money. Ironically, those who seem to be motivated by taking a great idea and turning it into reality are the ones who end up acquiring significant wealth.

In the last few years, we have taken this philosophy a step further. We have moved the headquarters and a substantial amount of the other pieces of our flagship business, as well as other businesses we are involved with, to downtown Detroit. An all-in commitment that our mission would not only be to continue to grow our business but also to help lead the transformation and rebuilding of one of America's most devastated urban centers.

And here is the secret sauce: **We are absolutely a more profitable (and better) business because we have a mission beyond the sole pursuit of profits.** The investment we make in the community with both our dollars and our team members' time has created a culture and environment that has motivated our people to be better at their day jobs. The yin feeds the yang, and the yang feeds the yin. You will attract the best and brightest who are motivated by more than a paycheck.

The more you invest in your mission, the more profits your business will produce. We are living proof of this. Not such a bad formula, huh?

BERRY GORDY

GENRE CREATOR: FOUNDER, MOTOWN RECORDS

Dr. Martin Luther King Jr. came to see me in Detroit at the peak of the civil rights era. And I was, of course, honored. He said, "What I'm trying to do politically and intellectually, you're doing with your music. I love the feeling people get when they hear your music. And so maybe we can make a deal." That was the biggest compliment I could think of. And we put out three albums covering his greatest speeches. It just goes to show that **if you do the right thing, the right thing will come to you.**

79

80

TERRY GOU

THE WORLD'S ELECTRONICS MAKER: FOUNDER, FOXCONN

In the first 20 years of my career, I worked hard to make money. It was necessary, because without it, accomplishing my ideals would not be possible.

In the second 20 years of my career, I worked for my ideals. Guided by those ideals and a purposeful life, I developed a good working spirit and self-confidence to withstand any challenge.

In the next 20 years, I will work for issues that are my passion. My interests and my priorities are using my life experience and what I have been able to achieve to nurture the next generation so they can make their own contributions to building a better world.

I believe that the most fortunate professionals in the world are those who can successfully carry out those three phases throughout their working life.

CARL ICAHN

CORPORATE RAIDER/ACTIVIST INVESTOR: FOUNDER, ICAHN ENTERPRISES

Sometimes the best way to make money is when most people say you are wrong and nuts. It's not easy to do, but it's like in the Rudyard Kipling poem: "if you can keep your head when all about you are losing theirs." **If you have the emotional makeup (you can develop it), you don't care what the experts are saying.**

You need to do a lot of work to be contrarian and you need to have the strength—you can't just be a contrarian to be contrarian. For example, when we had the junk bond crash of 1989, for a few days I was literally almost the only one buying—even though it took a few years, we made a fortune on them. I believed the risk-reward ratio was greatly in my favor because I felt I was buying companies, not bonds.

You are not always right, and it sometimes takes a long time to prove it out. A lot of the time you are early. (I really believe today, for example, that this market is going to have a crisis, some major corrections, so I have been hedged.) People thought I was crazy when I bought the Stratosphere Hotel in Las Vegas out of bankruptcy. It was in the north end of the Strip—at the time, a part of town as bad as a Third World country. Then I bought all the homes around the Stratosphere. Even the people in Las Vegas and at the hotel told me I was crazy. But it was the fact that I bought the shacks and the 24 acres next to the Stratosphere that made the hotel very attractive. Goldman Sachs ended up buying the Stratosphere from me, and we made about $1 billion.

It's not easy, but something inside you goes *click*. That's what I enjoy.

JERRY JONES

SCRAMBLER: OIL WILDCATTER, FOOTBALL REVOLUTIONARY; OWNER, DALLAS COWBOYS

In my mid-30s, I would have annual visits with Sam Walton. At that time I was primarily in the oil and gas business and some real estate. I asked him very early in our acquaintance if he had one rule that he practiced, what would it be, and I have applied it ever since. "If you are not undermanned, you're overstaffed, and you'll never see your heroes." What he meant: **Keep your labor or your expense down and maximize the responsibility you extend to fewer people.** When you do that you will see the people who have the ability and motivation to do the work.

When I bought the Cowboys in 1989, Tex Schramm had done a marvelous job creating visibility. What was lacking was the ability to monetize the visibility—to bring back home juice. When we first met, he said that football would be a hell of business if you didn't have to play those games. With Sam Walton in mind, I set out to have a franchise that could have financial viability, win or lose. I call it bringing the ten-pound bass in on the one-pound test line.

The ineffective people take care of themselves. Someone has to produce or it becomes apparent where they are. We need people with across-the-board knowledge in terms of what we are trying to do. One of the real plusses of oil and gas exploration is you can do it with a relatively small staff. We probably have only a dozen involved in running the Cowboys and related businesses. I am my own president and GM; if you eliminate my family you probably have only two or three people involved. You can do a lot of things with fewer people if you are willing to take a lot of risk. There is definitely a correlation.

SHAHID KHAN

**FACE OF THE AMERICAN DREAM:
OWNER, FLEX-N-GATE; OWNER,
JACKSONVILLE JAGUARS**

When I showed up in America at 16, I wasn't trying to make billions—I was just trying to survive. I had come from Pakistan with 500 bucks in my pocket and not much else. The bus dropped me off at a place that cost $8 a night. I asked if there was anything cheaper, and they told me to go to the YMCA. So I trudged down the street in the middle of one of the worst snowstorms in Illinois history. I had never seen snow before, and my shoes were falling apart. The YMCA cost $2 a night, and after a meal, I was already down $3 or $4. That was big money back in Pakistan.

But the next morning, I found an opportunity to make even bigger money. All I had to do was wash dishes and I could earn $1.20 an hour. That was more than 99% of the people back home in Pakistan. I realized right then that **this was the land of opportunity and I could control my own fate.** Less than 24 hours after arriving, I had already discovered the American Dream.

VINOD KHOSLA

LEADING LIGHT: COFOUNDER, FORMER CEO, SUN MICROSYSTEMS; VENTURE CAPITALIST (KLEINER PERKINS, KHOSLA VENTURES)

I explicitly don't build or guard my reputation. **I believe in telling it like it is and not worrying about it.**

CHARLES KOCH

THE POWER BROKER: INDUSTRIAL AND POLITICAL KINGPIN; CEO, KOCH INDUSTRIES

I expect all our employees to live up to the set of values that we started codifying for Koch Industries decades ago. Among our ten guiding principles: having integrity and humility, treating others with respect, proactively sharing knowledge and focusing on creating the greatest long-term value. The biggest mistake I've made in business is hiring and promoting executives who only paid lip service to them. That got us into several bad deals—and drove out people who shared our values. (It took several years to restructure our management teams and divest those deals.) **When hiring, if forced to choose between virtue and talent, choose virtue.** Talented people with bad values will do far more damage than virtuous people with lesser talents.

85

86

JEFF KOONS

RECORD-BREAKING ARTIST

People assume they are most creative at a certain age. But if you look at **truly great artists, they always get better.** Matisse got better. Picasso got better. Da Vinci got better. I think it's the same in all areas of creativity.

HENRY KRAVIS

ORIGINAL BARBARIAN: PRIVATE EQUITY PIONEER; COFOUNDER, KOHLBERG KRAVIS ROBERTS (KKR)

George Roberts and I are first cousins; we met at age 2 and we grew up together. We both went to Claremont McKenna College, and we roomed together in New York during summers, while I was working at Goldman Sachs and he at Bear Stearns. On our road trips from California to New York, we would quiz each other in the car: "What is yield? What's P/E?" We didn't know anything.

People often ask, "You must fight a lot?" The last fight we had was when we were 7 years old. He wanted to ride my new bike and I didn't want him to. He chased me in the house in Tulsa, and I ran into the corner of a wall, cracked my head open. I had 23 stitches and thought, "Well, there has to be a better way than this." So **we don't fight. We've never fought. We talk about things.** He doesn't agree with everything I think, and I don't agree with everything he thinks, nor should we. It's healthy. But we know each other so well I can finish his sentences, he can finish mine. Next to my wife, he is my best friend and confidant, and I trust him with my life, my family.

If you have the same values and are focused on the same goals, which is to build a firm that will be here long after we have retired, you can go a long way.

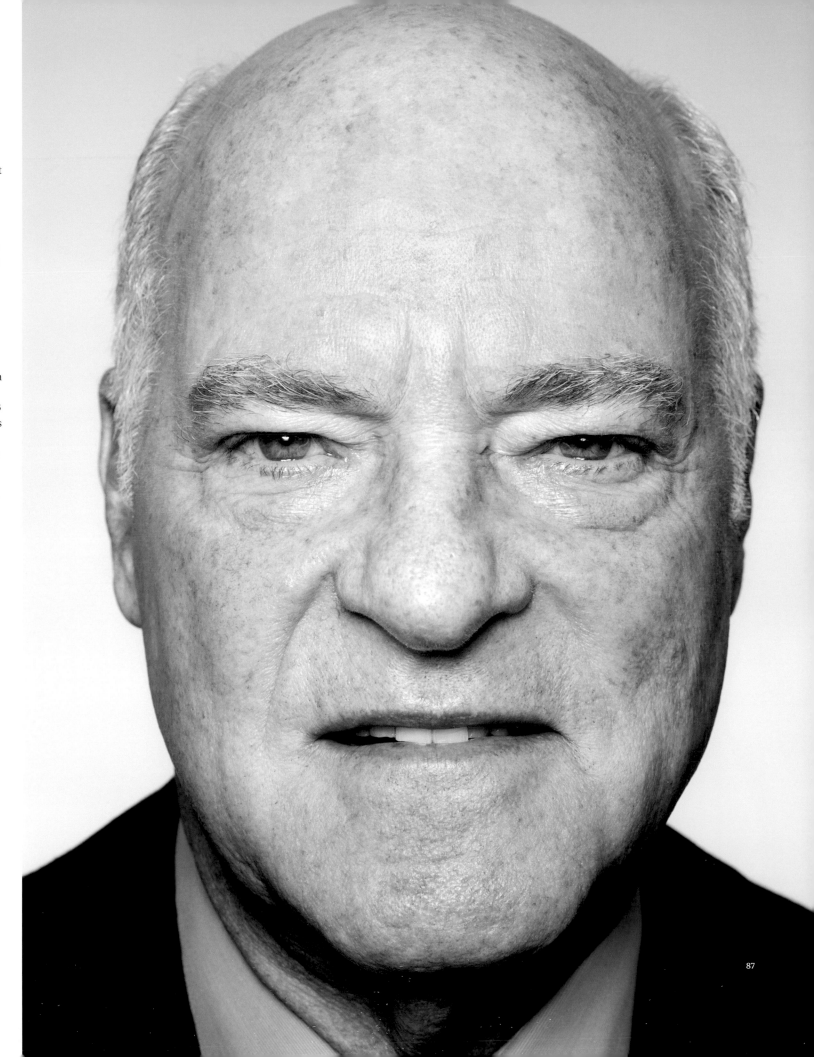

GUY LALIBERTÉ

SHOWMAN: BILLIONAIRE CO-FOUNDER, CIRQUE DU SOLEIL

I came up in Montreal as a street performer—a fire-breather, literally. I lived in the streets for almost ten years, by choice. And the streets have their own rules. Sometimes, **you have a fraction of a second to evaluate, when you first meet somebody, whether they might stab you or become your friend.** The things I learned in the street about reading and feeling people and believing my intuition proved very important in my business life. If I was entering a meeting, I was able to stand and scan people and feel them immediately as what they were, instead of discovering weeks later, when it was too late.

LEE SHAU KEE

**HONG KONG'S LANDLORD;
STOCK-PICKING SAVANT**

There's a Chinese saying: **"Explore
what's best in the others and
follow."** Among my friends, I
always learn the best from them.

89

LI KA-SHING

ASIA'S SUPERMAN: CHAIRMAN, CK HUTCHISON AND CHEUNG KONG PROPERTY; RESPECTED PHILANTHROPIST

My experience in manufacturing taught me cash flow is the lifeblood of a company and one of the best safeguards for a company's future. Between 1999 and 2000, when everyone saw the 3G development in Europe as a gold mine, it was overhyped. All through the spectrum auction, I directed our team to adhere to our cash flow projection and only advance with cautious deliberation. I knew **everyone thought I was too conservative** and challenged this mandate. But in retrospect our telecom businesses remain competitive while several of those companies that won the bid were stuck. Writing a check to invest $100 is easy; returning the same to shareholders is harder. That's why I am a strong believer in advancing with cautious deliberation. Prudence and agility, creativity and innovation will give you the edge to thrive in uncertain times.

PETER LYNCH

AMERICA'S MONEY MANAGER: FORMER PORTFOLIO MANAGER, MAGELLAN FUND

My biggest mistake was that I always sold stocks way too early. In fact, I got a call from Warren Buffett in 1989. My daughter picks up the phone and says, "It's Mr. Buffett on the line." And I thought some of my buddies are kidding me because she was only 6. And I pick up the phone, and I hear, "This is Warren Buffett from Omaha, Nebraska." You know, he talks so fast. "And I love your book, *One Up on Wall Street*, and I want to use a line from it in my year-end report. I have to have it. Can I please use it?" I said, "Sure. What's the line?" He says, "Selling your winners and holding your losers is like cutting the flowers and watering the weeds."

That one line that he picked in my whole book has been my greatest mistake. I visited the first four Home Depots ever built. I sold that stock after it tripled, and then it went up another fiftyfold. **If you're great in this business you're right six times out of ten.** But the times you're right, if you make a triple or ten-bagger, it overcomes your mistakes. So you have to find the big winners. I sold way too early on Home Depot. I sold too early on Dunkin' Donuts. Why did I do that? I was dumb. With great companies the passage of time is a major positive.

BERNARD MARCUS

BUILDER: COFOUNDER, HOME DEPOT

Age is just a number for me—I haven't thought about it in years. I go by the motto that I learn something new every single day. From reading and asking questions, you broaden your knowledge, your thinking, every aspect of your life. **By the end of the day, I've learned something that shows how dumb I was yesterday.**

J.W. "BILL" MARRIOTT JR.

AMERICA'S HOTELIER: CHAIRMAN, MARRIOTT INTERNATIONAL

I learned what may be the single biggest factor in our success the hard way, when I was in the Navy. I was assigned to be the wardroom officer on an aircraft carrier, and I had a bunch of stewards doing the food preparation. They were enlisted men who were World War II veterans because this was back in the early 1950s. I had new recipe cards that I thought would improve the quality of the food. I gave them an order to follow the cards. And they just gave me this glassy stare and said, "We ain't following them," and I didn't know what to do, so I let them do their own thing. I realized that I didn't get their buy-in. I didn't sit down with them and say, I think we can improve the quality of the food if you follow these recipes.

The four most important words in business are "What do you think?" And that's why I would visit over 200 hotels a year to meet with our associates. You can talk about all the technology, distribution and other things that are taking place. If you take good care of your associates, they'll take good care of the customers and the customers will come back. We're in the people business. We don't manufacture anything. We just take care of our guests.

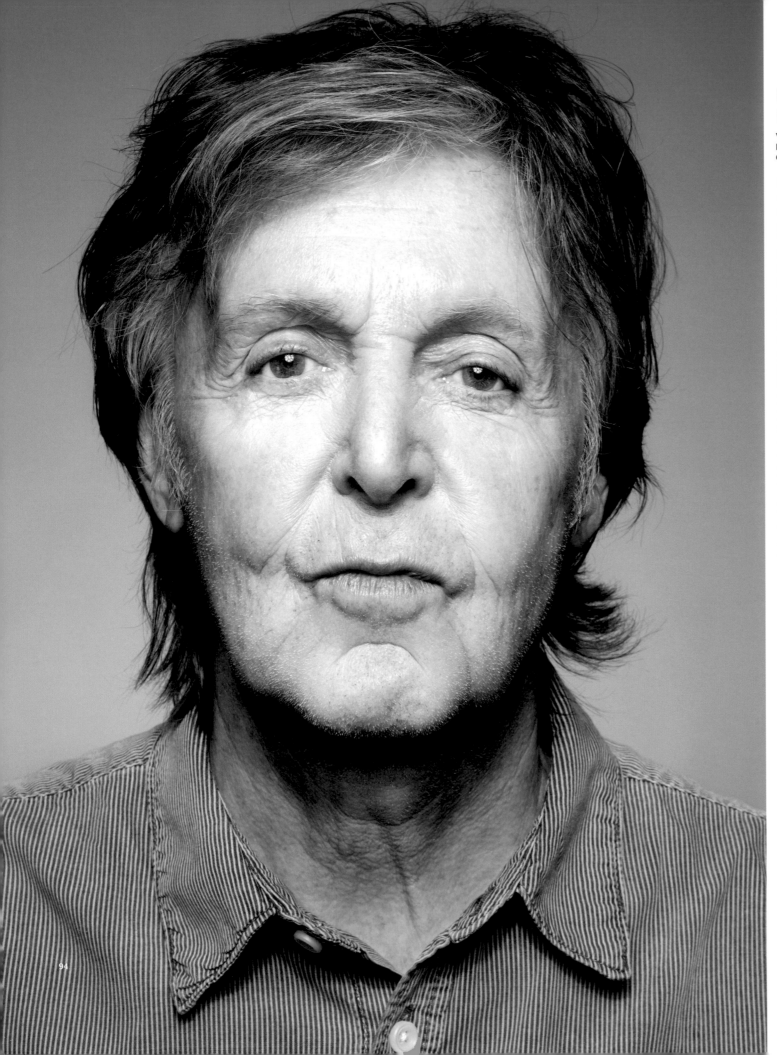

PAUL MCCARTNEY

**VOICE OF A GENERATION:
BEATLE, ARTIST, SONGWRITER,
COPYRIGHT OWNER**

In the mid-1980s, Michael Jackson and I were hanging out, and he asked me for career advice. I said, "Okay, three things: First of all, get yourself a really good manager. You're really hot now, there's going to be a lot of money coming in, and you really need someone to help you manage it. Second, think about getting into videos." (Shortly after that, he did "Thriller," so I thought that was cool, he took my advice.) Then I said, "And finally, be careful about your songs—own your work—and get into song publishing." And he said, "Oh, I'm going to get yours!" I kind of laughed; I didn't think he was serious. But he was.

It all goes back to the very beginning of the Beatles, when we signed the music publishing contract. We didn't care what it was: We were just like any other writers; we wanted to get published. It turned out to be basically a slave contract; no matter how successful we made the company, we didn't get a raise. After John died, I talked to Sir Lew Grade, who owned Northern Songs, the company that held our publishing rights. I said, "Lew, if you're ever going to sell Northern Songs, you've got to come to me first." He said, "I'm never going to sell." And I said, "Fair enough. But if you do, come to me first." He later came to me and said, "Yeah, I am selling it—for $20 million." I said, "Okay, I think that's a fair valuation."

But I didn't want to be the guy who bought John out. So I went to John's people, and I said, "We've got this opportunity to buy Northern Songs, finally. It's $20 million. And so that's $10 million from me, $10 million from you. And we should do this, what do you think?" The response: "Oh, no, we can get it for $4 million." I said, "I'm not sure about that." It ended up falling through, and Michael later ended up buying it off this Australian guy Robert Holmes à Court for $47.5 million. I wasn't willing to pay that much for my own songs. **It's difficult, when you've written them for nothing, to pay $50 million to get them back.**

It's so important to have good people around you. That's why I'm anywhere near this list. My lawyers, John and Lee Eastman, are really smart, both great guys, and I listen to them. In recent years, they've helped me recover my copyrights. (There's a U.S. law that allows me to get them back.) If I'm wheeling and dealing, life becomes very difficult for me. I've got to reserve a portion of my brain for writing songs.

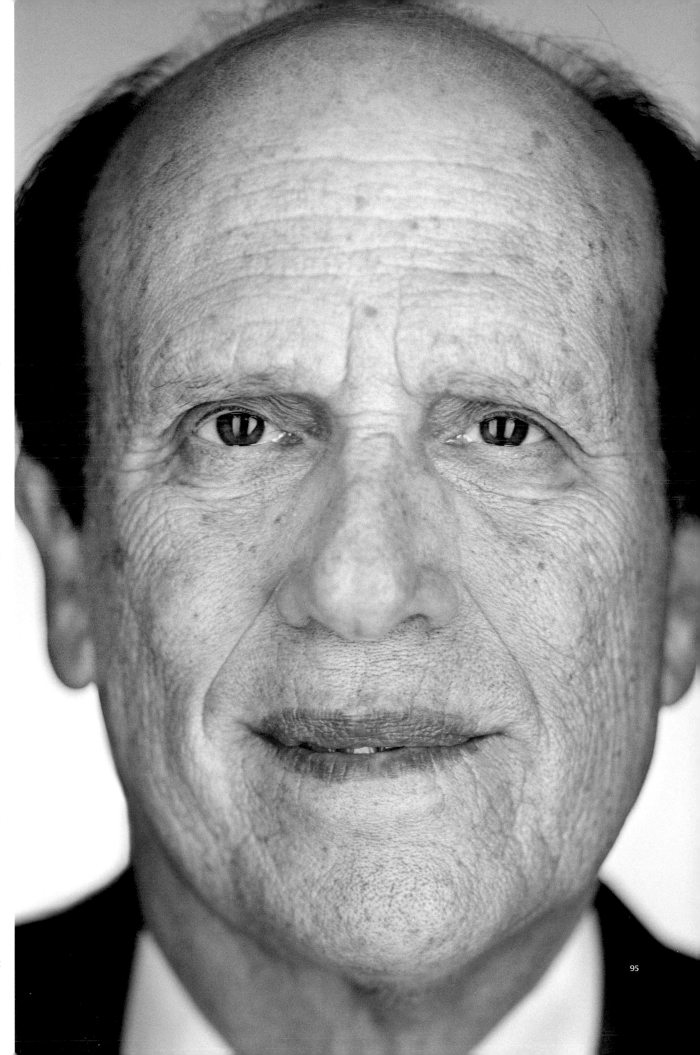

MICHAEL MILKEN

**FINANCIAL ALCHEMIST: JUNK-BOND
PRODIGY (DREXEL BURNHAM LAMBERT),
WALL STREET POSTER CHILD, PHILANTHROPIST**

I came of age and went into business right in the middle of these past 100 years. Two issues of *Forbes* had a particularly significant influence on me: the 50th anniversary issue, in 1967, and the 60th anniversary issue ten years later. I carried the latter in a briefcase for years and reread it often.

Both issues really made me think about how financial structures changed over time and how leading companies changed. I often point out that automobiles changed the world, but in 1917, when the majority of a car's cost was based on raw materials, the country's largest company by far was U.S. Steel. Other top companies included International Harvester, U.S. Rubber, Anaconda Copper and Phelps Dodge—so you can see how natural resources dominated society. A century later, these resources make up only a tiny fraction of the cost of the dominant product, the microchip, whose primary economic input is the brainpower of engineers.

A century ago, the automobile was radically changing transportation and mobility. Ford Motor was the 21st-largest company. By the time it went public in 1956 with what was then the largest stock sale in history, it was one of the most valuable companies in the U.S. Today its total market value is less than the annual price variation of Amazon, Facebook, Apple or Google.

Understanding how change occurs is key. By the 1970s, Singer, the sewing-machine maker, was known for an unbroken record of paying dividends going back more than 100 years. But that wasn't as relevant as the emancipation of women, which had been upending its business for years. The company didn't understand that women were less interested in sewing than in careers.

I was in elementary school in the 1950s when Sputnik went up. That made me think about science, and I later went to Berkeley because it had so many scientific Nobel laureates. Before the 1965 Watts Riot, I thought the American Dream was achievable without regard to race. When I found that it wasn't, I switched my major from science to business. Twenty-two years later, I helped finance Reginald Lewis, the Jackie Robinson of the business world, when he bought Beatrice International Foods from Beatrice Cos. for $985 million. **Finance can change the world and create millions of jobs by empowering people with ability.**

Today's growing challenge: create meaningful lives for the world's population. We've accomplished the greatest achievement of mankind, the extension of life. Over 4 million years of evolution, life expectancy of early hominids and then Homo sapiens had only increased from about 20 to 31. But just since 1900, average human life expectancy worldwide has grown from 31 to over 70. Economists estimate that about half of economic growth is tied to the public health and medical research advances that underlie increased longevity.

How do you create meaningful lives for all these people, and the 1 to 2 billion more who will soon be living? What are the jobs of the future in an age of robotics, driverless trucks and other new technologies? At one point, 90% of Americans worked in agriculture, then 40% and now less than 2%. U.S. Steel was the number one company a century ago, but today the American steel industry directly employs fewer than 140,000 workers. It's a great challenge.

Most people who build businesses are passionate about it. They stand for something. The people who worked with me believed, as I do, in the democratization of capital—an opportunity to empower talent and help job creation in America. My legacy isn't any one asset class like junk bonds. It's the understanding of capital structure and how best to finance companies that create jobs and drive change.

95

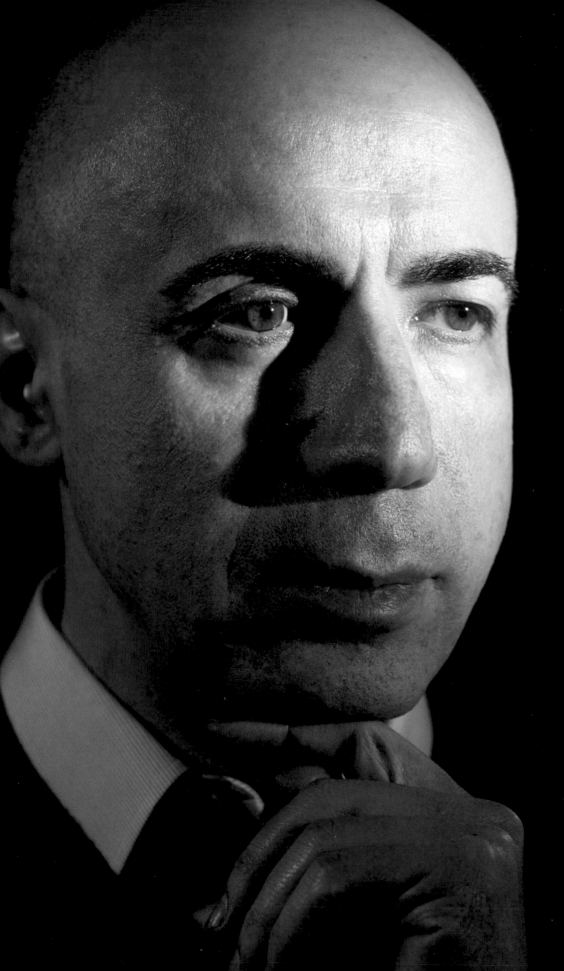

YURI MILNER

RUSSIA'S TECH SUCCESS STORY: BILLIONAIRE FOUNDER, DST GLOBAL; INVESTED IN FACEBOOK, AIRBNB, TWITTER, ETC.

On November 21, 1783, Benjamin Franklin watched as the first manned hot-air balloon rose from the ground. A skeptic in the crowd called out, "What is the use of it?" And Franklin is said to have replied, "What is the use of a newborn child?" He had a vision of humanity not as it was but as it could be. And he understood that from each new height a new horizon comes into view. That's what matters most. When I was growing up in the Soviet Union, **my father told me if I wanted to learn about business, I had to start looking beyond my horizon,** at least as far as America.

Most of the better decisions I've made in my career came from trying to look beyond the horizon. The first was in the '90s, betting everything on the internet. I believed it would be one of the most profound advances for civilization since electricity. I built one of the biggest internet startups in Europe, then founded DST Global, an investment firm targeting internet companies worldwide. The key to our investment philosophy is to support founders, enabling progress through technology.

Four years ago, I joined with Mark Zuckerberg and Priscilla Chan, Sergey Brin and Anne Wojcicki to found the Breakthrough Prize, the world's biggest award for fundamental science and mathematics. We believe these are the best tools we have for understanding the universe and advancing our civilization. Then, last year, Mark joined with me and Stephen Hawking to launch Breakthrough Starshot, the first practical attempt to reach another star. As Franklin understood, the higher we go, the wider our horizons become — and the bigger the challenge of looking beyond them. Breakthrough Starshot, if it succeeds, could set our horizon at the interstellar scale.

LAKSHMI MITTAL

WORLD BUILDER: CHAIRMAN, CEO, ARCELORMITTAL, THE LARGEST STEELMAKER ON EARTH

Steel is one of the most used materials in the world today, but that doesn't mean in the future there won't be a different way of making steel or that other, new materials won't be developed that challenge steel's position. The pace of technological change is significantly faster than historically—**every industry today has to fight complacency,** prepare to see the disruption coming and then be flexible enough to adapt swiftly.

97

PATRICE MOTSEPE

**ENTREPRENEURIAL ICON:
AFRICA'S FIRST BLACK
BILLIONAIRE**

After I completed my first significant transaction, buying mines that were closed or about to close, with a demotivated workforce of 8,000, who for years had been told, "Guys, you're not cutting it," people asked if I was mad. But we ran our business differently and it worked—**we paid our workers based on profitability,** with bonuses based on aspirational targets that, if achieved, created money for the mine workers, the company and its shareholders alike.

RUPERT MURDOCH

LAST OF THE NEWSPAPER MOGULS, SHREWDEST OF THE POWER BROKERS: EXECUTIVE CHAIRMAN, NEWS CORP., 21ST CENTURY FOX

As a relatively shy and inexperienced young newspaper owner at the *Adelaide News* in Australia, I was lucky enough to work alongside top-notch reporters, editors, compositors who put together the paper in metal form ahead of its printing. Hardy souls who had no time for elitism or airs and graces, and even less time for incompetence.

My outlook, energy, self-assurance and sense of social purpose were fashioned in the slightly mad meritocracy that is the newsroom, where you start each day with a blank canvas and relentlessly strive to capture as much original news as possible and present it in a manner that is coherent, compelling and valuable. The urgency, daily drive, that constant self-questioning integral in editing a paper, the ceaseless curiosity, are what I have stood upon every day of my career, taking me and our businesses further than my young self ever imagined. Those experiences, those principles, helped me build a business in television and films and digital media, where drive and creativity are essential and working as part of a team, regardless of your title, is imperative.

To those early colleagues, who tolerated my inexperience and guided me with their earthy wisdom, I am and will always be grateful.

ELON MUSK

**IRON MAN: ALPHA ENTREPRENEUR;
COFOUNDER, PAYPAL, TESLA,
SPACEX**

Artificial intelligence will provide many societal benefits, including self-driving cars and improved medical diagnostics. However, with AI we may be summoning the demon and could create an existential risk to humanity. If a digital superintelligence were inadvertently optimized to do something detrimental to humanity, this could have catastrophic consequences. It could be something like directing the AI to get rid of spam, and it concludes the best way to get rid of spam is to get rid of humans. Or a financial program decides the best way to make money is to increase the value of defense stocks by starting a war. **We're the first species capable of self-annihilation, and it's extremely likely, given enough time.** The question: Can we get ahead of it? We need to learn as much as possible and should create a government agency to regulate AI. Ultimately the private sector will have to take the lead in building safe and useful technology that benefits humanity.

JACQUELINE NOVOGRATZ

SOCIAL CAPITALIST: FOUNDER, ACUMEN FUND

In our connected era, word spreads. People know when you are being true to your values. **Don't worry about reputation but about character.** You build character by practicing empathy, practicing moral courage, practicing determination. Those traits are like muscles. When you are known for that, you don't have to worry about guarding your reputation—others will do it for you.

101

SEAN PARKER

AGENT OF DISRUPTION: NAPSTER COFOUNDER, FACEBOOK'S FIRST PRESIDENT, SPOTIFY EVANGELIST

I've been involved in the start of many innovative ideas and companies, not because they were fashionable at the time but because they appealed to my sense of intellectual curiosity. Just as experts in the record industry couldn't accept that music on the internet would ever go mainstream, or that social media would ever be used by adults rather than college kids, **I have always chosen to ignore the conventional wisdom in favor of the ideas that interested me.** Inventing the future starts with intellectual curiosity—along with a healthy dose of skepticism. You need enough curiosity to "deep dive" into the ideas that interest you. And enough skepticism to second-guess everything you think you know and everything the so-called experts want you to believe.

We're living at a unique moment in history, where everyone on the internet who has a knack for Googling can access more information than any university could ever teach. About a decade ago I became interested in the emerging field of cancer immunotherapy. The data was compelling, even though the field had been written off by famous oncologists. But with little more than the internet at my disposal, I was able to learn enough about the field to be dangerous. I got involved in funding clinical trials for drugs that would ultimately treat blood cancers and melanoma.

In a few short years the field of immunotherapy had produced several billion-dollar companies, FDA-approved drugs and breakthroughs that helped patients where conventional treatments had failed. I launched a nonprofit institute dedicated to the field, assembling a dream team of scientists around a $250 million bet that the next generation of immunotherapy treatments would treat an even larger number of patients. While engineering T cells to fight cancer may seem very different from writing software to give away free music, the instincts that led me to each of these projects haven't changed a bit.

JAMES PATTERSON

WRITER OF LITERATURE AT SCALE: RECORD-SETTING AUTHOR (87 NO. 1 BESTSELLERS); FORMER CEO, J. WALTER THOMPSON

Don't take "no" when your gut tells you "yes." Just before Little, Brown published *Along Came a Spider,* the first of my Alex Cross books, I said I wanted to do a TV commercial. They said, "We don't do TV commercials." So I just went and did one for nothing—$1,500. And then I brought it to them, and they went, "Ooh, we like this." I said, "Let's run it." That started things going. The book and me went on the bestsellers list.

Once I got out of the advertising business, I had a lot more time. I remember going to my publisher, saying, "I want to do more than one book a year." I told them one was at a beach house, and it was a mystery. And the other one was *Suzanne's Diary for Nicholas.* The fellow who ran Time Warner said, "We want to do *The Beach House,* but we don't want to do *Suzanne's Diary* because it's not your brand." And I went, "**I don't think of myself as a brand. But if I did, I think the brand is when you pick up a James Patterson book, the pages are really going to fly for you.**" It was a big moment in my career because it was the point at which I went from publishing one book a year to ultimately 20. And in multiple genres.

I faced the same resistance when I started writing children's books. People have a tendency to stay within their comfort zone, and many thought I could only do adult thrillers. I knew I could write great kids' books, though, and launched my own children's imprint, JIMMY Patterson. Now I publish nearly as many kids' bestsellers as I do adult titles.

RONALD PERELMAN

REVLON RON; BUYOUT SPECIALIST

The world is changing so fast that you cannot bask in any sort of passivity, because it doesn't exist anymore. You have to be on top of your game at all times. Two kids can develop Google in their garage, and 15 years later, it's the most powerful company in the world. **It's like the Henry Ford days on steroids.** Everything today is speed, and there is always somebody else working on something better. One of our companies, Deluxe, was the largest supplier of prints to the film industry. We knew that prints was declining but didn't know it was about to go off a cliff.

Luckily, we were already supplying a digital solution for the same service, but a transition that we thought would take years only took a matter of weeks.

H. ROSS PEROT

DATA PIONEER (EDS, PEROT SYSTEMS); THE ORIGINAL POPULIST-BUSINESSMAN PRESIDENTIAL CANDIDATE

Believe in big ideas. In 1962 I was IBM's biggest salesman for those giant mainframe computers. I tried to convince IBM we were missing an opportunity, that in addition to selling the computers, we ought to sell services, too—as in help our customers learn how to use their new machines. But IBM wasn't interested, and my big idea nearly died right there.

That week I went to get my hair cut, and while flipping through a *Reader's Digest* I came across a quote from Henry David Thoreau: "The mass of men lead lives of quiet desperation." That wasn't for me. **It was at that moment that I decided to go it alone, to start my own company**, Electronic Data Systems. After 70 sales calls I finally landed my first customer.

Two decades later, after I had sold EDS to General Motors, I got into the business of backing the next generation of entrepreneurs. I recognized a little bit of myself in 1986 when I put up $20 million to seed Steve Jobs at NeXT Computer, which he eventually sold to Apple Computer. He believed in big ideas, too.

T. BOONE PICKENS

RISK-TAKER: OIL WILDCATTER, HEDGE FUND MANAGER

Over the Christmas holiday, I had several strokes, and in June, I suffered a Texas-size fall that required hospitalization. I am still mentally strong, and I comprehend and process information like I did before the incident, but sometimes find myself literally at a loss for words. That's been tough for a loudmouth like me, as I've always believed you can trace every problem to a lack of communication or lack of clarity in communication.

Many of those who face adversity like this at 89 choose to hide it. My life has always been an open book. Some chapters of my life have been great. Others not so much. I clearly am in the fourth quarter, and the clock is ticking, and my health is in decline. Now, don't for a minute think I'm being morbid. When you're in the oil business like I've been all my life, **you drill your fair share of dry holes, but you never lose your optimism.** There's a story I tell about the geologist who fell off a ten-story building. When he blew past the fifth floor he thought to himself, "So far, so good." That's the way to approach life. Be the eternal optimist who is excited to see what the next decade will bring. I thrive on that, and I'm going to stick to it until the game is over.

MIUCCIA PRADA

**INFLUENTIAL DESIGNER:
CO-CEO, PRADA**

I'm not really interested in building a reputation for myself. But I do
care for what the company stands
for. **I believe in work and being
connected to the world we live in.**
You need to be curious and never
stop studying. You have to challenge yourself to think every day
to understand and react to what is
happening.

SHONDA RHIMES

**TELEVISIONARY: HOLLYWOOD'S
TOP SHOWRUNNER**

Storytelling has become ubiquitous,
across so many mediums, creating
an audience that's ever more sophisticated. But it doesn't matter how
many people tell stories or how many
platforms they go on. Storytelling remains basic: **It's a just a campfire, the
human connection that says** *you're
not alone.*

New mediums like VR will go so far as
to put you inside, but there's going to
be a lot of dissatisfaction there. If you
decide the ending, there's no adven-
ture. In a world of unlimited voices
and choices, those who can bring
people together and tell a good story
have power.

JULIAN ROBERTSON

HEDGE FUND GODFATHER: FOUNDER, TIGER MANAGEMENT

Do you know what the most desirable job was at the beginning of my career, in the 1950s? Advertising. All the hotshots went into advertising. Investment banks? They were begging for people. I was interested in stocks from an early age, so I really wanted to go into investment banking. The fancy way in was to go to business school and then get into the investment banking department of one of the firms, but I started as a stockbroker.

Today, people wonder why hedge funds aren't doing better—I think it is from increasing competition from other hedge funds. **If I were starting out now, I would look at what the competition is like in various fields—and then consider some that aren't so popular.**

MARTINE ROTHBLATT

PERPETUAL REINVENTOR: FOUNDER, SIRIUS, UNITED THERAPEUTICS; CREATOR OF PANAMSAT

Anything worthwhile in life requires teamwork, and you cannot manage what you don't understand. My favorite thing to do at work is to walk around and talk to people. Each person is like a library of information. The more I know about a person, the better able I am to connect them to other people with synergistic interests—**a leader works for those they lead.** Lawrence Bell, the founder of Bell Aircraft, said that anyone unwilling to do small things should not be trusted to do big things. Running a business is a very big thing, because you are having an outsize effect on countless people's lives. Hence, when I started creating organ-manufacturing technology, I practiced suturing arteries.

I find it awe-inspiring that there are an infinite number of ways to improve the world through business. Providing better products and services, or less expensive ones, or more accessible ones, all makes people happier. That's what it's all about.

DAVID M. RUBENSTEIN

**WASHINGTON'S FINANCIER:
COFOUNDER, CO-CEO,
THE CARLYLE GROUP**

Thomas Jefferson famously said that the country is, to some extent, about the pursuit of happiness. Unfortunately, over the next 50 years of his life he never defined what happiness was. Personal happiness might be the most elusive thing in life. In my own case, personal happiness came about much more from giving away my money than from earning it. I use what I call the "mother test." **If your mother calls you and tells you that she is proud of what you are doing, that's probably a good indication** that you are on the road to happiness. My mother used to call much more when I was giving away my money than when I was making it.

SHERYL SANDBERG

TECH TRAILBLAZER: WOMEN'S LEADERSHIP CHAMPION; COO, FACEBOOK

Driving to work on my first day back after maternity leave, I cried the entire way there. I wanted to work, but leaving my son at home was hard. To be able to see him, I started finding ways to come in later and leave earlier.

Years later I mentioned in an interview that I left work at 5:30. The response was overwhelmingly positive. That's when I realized that **we are better employees when we stop trying to be two people and bring our whole selves to work.** That doesn't mean working around the clock. It means sharing what you are going through so that other people can empathize and help you.

When I lost my husband Dave two years ago, I learned this lesson even more deeply. Dave was a true partner at home and at work and taught me the value of peer mentorship. When I was talking to Mark about joining Facebook, Dave told me not to work out the substance in advance but rather to agree on the process. His point was that the substance would change but our working relationship was the single most important thing to get right. We agreed to sit together, giving each other feedback every week one-on-one. Nine years later, I often smile when I remember how Dave's advice set us up for success.

So bringing my full self to work meant being openly sad. The way colleagues supported me drove home the need for better policies for bereavement and sick leave. Taking care of people when they need it most is not just the right thing to do, it is the smart thing to do.

ERIC SCHMIDT

THE ADULT IN THE ROOM: FORMER CEO, CHAIRMAN, NOVELL; FORMER CEO, GOOGLE

In 2001, my friend and colleague John Doerr called to suggest that I get some coaching. What? I was far along in my career; I didn't need a coach. I could *be* a coach. Of course, I was wrong about that. I actually needed the coach.

We all called the late Bill Campbell "Coach," and it wasn't because of the 2-41-1 record he compiled as the head coach of the Columbia football team in the late '70s. He knew what was needed to succeed—to win—in Silicon Valley.

Bill wasn't some far-off guru who didn't get his hands dirty, but a coach who got on the playing field with me. He participated in board and executive meetings, developing credibility with my management team and helping us make crucial decisions. He would give advice and then make sure I lived by it. I would spend hours in his small office—whiteboards, markers, etc.—going over the "plays." Without fail, he knew what I needed to do, and he knew how I should do it.

Bill had many tenets of leadership, but one that sticks with me, especially at this moment, is to **"maintain a culture of respect."** This was essential for him—and he knew it came from the top of any organization. I worked hard to make sure that the prevailing culture at Google was one of respect above all else, as Larry and Sergey always have, and as Sundar does today. Like much of Coach's advice, this one continues to resonate. I miss my coach.

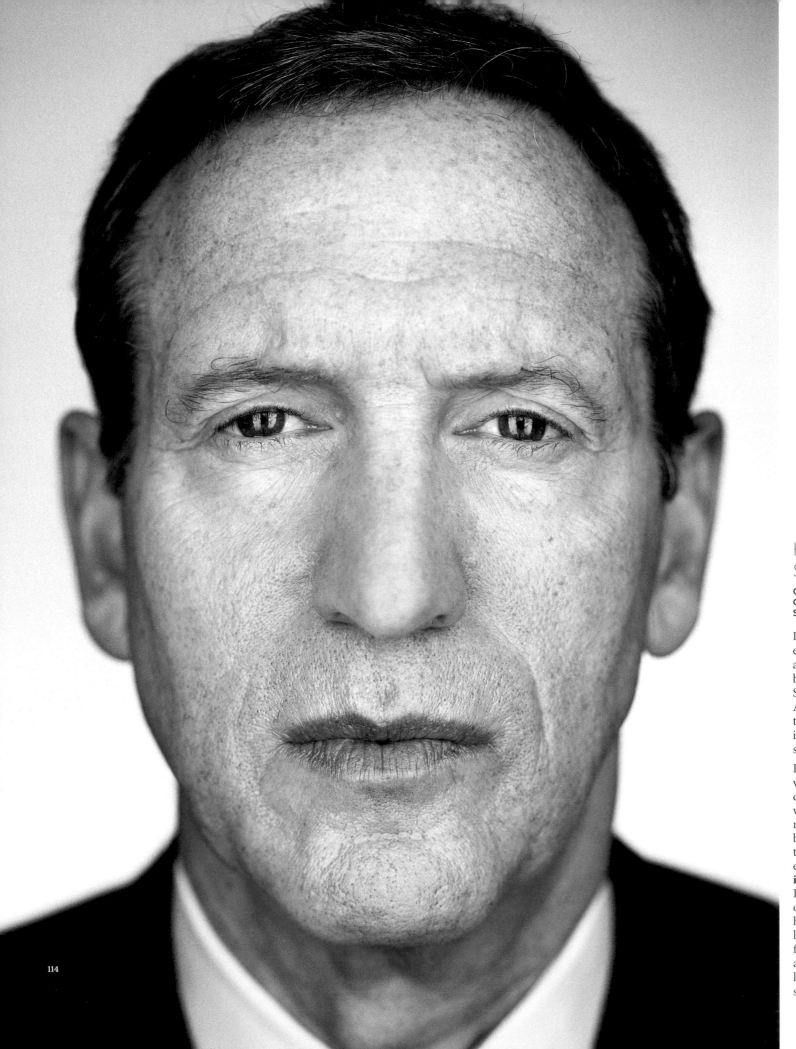

HOWARD SCHULTZ

COFFEE CZAR: EXECUTIVE CHAIRMAN, FORMER CEO, STARBUCKS

In 1987, we had 11 stores and 100 employees and were already speaking about the need for a business to balance profitability and benevolence. Starbucks was one of the first American companies to give part-time workers comprehensive health insurance and equity in the form of stock options.

Back then our shareholders were very angry and concerned about dilution. I convinced them that we would be more profitable, more productive, by creating these benefits. When we made college tuition free a few years ago, I explained it wasn't charity because **investing in people is how we grow.** I'm still trying to build the kind of company that my father never had a chance to work for; he held lots of blue-collar jobs, and I saw firsthand what being disrespected and devalued did to him. He had no loyalty to any employer because they showed no loyalty to him.

CHARLES SCHWAB

BROKERAGE DEMOCRATIZER: FOUNDER, CHARLES SCHWAB

In the late 1990s and early 2000s, we were growing by leaps and bounds. Everybody wanted to trade stocks. Then came the dot-com bust, and all of a sudden, business collapsed. I came back as CEO in 2004. **We realized success had covered over mistakes, and we had begun to lose our compass.** The only path forward was to go back to our core values—helping individual investors with lower costs, less complexity and great service. We cut expenses, we trimmed back staff, we sold off businesses and ultimately we turned things around.

STEPHEN SCHWARZMAN

**PRIVATE EQUITY KINGPIN:
COFOUNDER, BLACKSTONE**

When Pete Peterson and I launched Blackstone in 1985, we wanted to create a place where people would enjoy coming to work and be rewarded for internal collaboration. The firm we came from was known for its internal rivalries, with partners often at odds, plotting against and one-upping each other.

Creating this environment became important early in Blackstone's history, as we moved from M&A into private equity. We had no organization then. People would just come into my office and ask me to make decisions. One deal, a steel distribution company in Philadelphia called Edgcomb Steel, didn't turn out the way we hoped because we failed to solicit multiple points of view from all of our partners. I had a special tombstone made for that deal, which was black and in the shape of an actual tombstone to remind myself every day of what I learned. I realized that **we needed to set up rigorous processes to review deals together** and help avoid risks, even if that meant challenging an idea I was putting forward. Nobody's job was to say, "I think it's wonderful." Instead, I insisted on everyone coming together to analyze potential problems that could lose investor money.

Today we've institutionalized this approach across the firm and have our deal teams meet every Monday to review each potential transaction. We've replicated this process across each of our business groups. Without this process, I'm not sure we would have evolved into a successful business.

NEIL SHEN

**CHINA'S PREEMINENT
VENTURE CAPITALIST**

Our business changes so quickly that one must continuously go through learning curves to stay relevant. **A part of learning is done through reading, and the other part, which is likely more important, is talking with bright minds from different fields**—scientists, writers, policy-makers, philosophers, etc. Such engagement helps you get many new perspectives on life and the world.

We are in the business of helping entrepreneurs build the very best companies in the world, mostly in the technology space. I do not think we will be replaced by AI. This business oftentimes is more like art than science.

We might have to live with an easy monetary policy environment on a global basis for a very long period of time to come. How to consistently create value and generate alpha, with this backdrop, is the real challenge.

117

RUSSELL SIMMONS

HIP-HOP PIONEER; SERIAL ENTREPRENEUR; YOGA GURU

The self is the greatest teacher: The more you dig, the more you learn. So the **self-discovery is your journey.** Yogis refer to the state of yoga, which is the same as heaven on Earth. If you're present and awake, you become this great thinker, this great worker. You become a fine-tuned machine.

CHAROEN SIRIVADHANABHAKDI

**ASIAN CONGLOMERATOR:
FOUNDER, THAI BEVERAGE**

As a child, I saw my parents making preparations for their hoi tod (crispy pan-fried mussels in egg batter) store from before dawn until midnight every day, yet still make time to teach their 11 children to be diligent, responsible and grateful to those who had helped and cared for us. If I could turn back time, I would like to create a right balance in life. I think I have done better than in the past by dedicating some time to looking after my health and my quality of life. My wife always reminds me of the following truths in life: **Health is your own; money belongs to others; power is temporary; and reputation is eternal.** That is why I teach my children to find the right balance between working to build up business and maintaining good health.

JEFF SKOLL

IMPACT MAN: EBAY BILLIONAIRE; SOCIAL ENTREPRENEURSHIP KINGPIN

We are on the cusp of a clean-energy economy, where energy is essentially costless, abundant and safe, with no externalities, no health costs, no Deepwater Horizons. Around the world, solar has done what looks like Moore's Law. Wind has done somewhat the same, coming down to a competitive place. And to finish the trifecta, there's a step change in batteries about to hit the world next year. I would liken the clean-energy revolution to the industrial revolution, just happening faster. The numbers are staggering.

Having **clean, inexpensive, sufficient energy that's not controlled in some government's hands or some big business' hands helps solve a couple of the giant threats** coming down the pike. Climate change, obviously, is a biggie— this stuff doesn't solve it, but it mitigates it. In terms of water issues, if you have enough clean energy and you have access to an ocean, you can desalinate and then pipe that desalinated water where you need it, and grow food in deserts that previously couldn't sustain agriculture. In the Middle East, there's a lot of conflict over water as well as refugees and displacement. Clean tech may also cover some of the issues with nuclear proliferation. There's no need to build new nuclear plants, so why would anyone build one except for weapons? On the pandemics side, people living in better living conditions with more plentiful health and food options are less likely to be struck with diseases that become epidemics that become pandemics.

The clean-energy economy can happen in the next 10 years. So when I think out 100 years, we're either going to be in a world of extreme abundance and peace and prosperity where people live these glorious lives, or we're going to be toast. It's one or the other.

120

CARLOS SLIM HELÚ

MEXICO'S ONE-MAN ECONOMY; ONETIME RICHEST MAN IN THE WORLD

At the end we leave with nothing. Entrepreneurs are only temporary managers of wealth. So **do right by your customers, your employees, your backers.**

121

FRED SMITH

THE WORLD OVERNIGHT: FOUNDER, FEDEX

Everything was going as planned in the early days of FedEx, until the Arab oil embargo hit in 1973. Suddenly our costs spiked and our cash evaporated. Right around then I went out to Vegas with this high roller I knew. We went to the casino and he got me a line of credit.

I knew how to play blackjack from my days in Vietnam. It was a horrible war with a bad strategy and terrible consequences, but I met some great people and played a lot of cards. The odds in blackjack actually aren't that bad if you know how to bet. The problem is most people get chicken and pull their money off the table exactly when they ought to be doubling down. I didn't have that problem.

I won $27,000 and wired it back to the company. The myth says that money alone saved FedEx. The truth is that we owed so much damn money, $27,000 didn't make much of a difference on the balance sheet. But it lifted our confidence at a time that we needed it. No business school graduate would recommend gambling as a financial strategy, but **sometimes it pays to be a little crazy early in your career.**

ROBERT SMITH

**PRIVATE EQUITY BILLIONAIRE:
FOUNDER, VISTA EQUITY PARTNERS**

My training as a chemical engineer sharpened my passion for complex systems—tor understanding them, deconstructing them and finding their equilibrium. But while **I found beauty in the absolute truth of machines in the classroom, I found purpose in the messiness of human interactions** in the real world. Whatever drives us, we all derive happiness from finding purpose. We find joy in thinking, doing and discovering—in improving people's lives and catalyzing positive change in the world. And in this age of intellectual capital, where brainpower is the world's most valued currency, the opportunity to find purpose—and create value that aligns with our values—has never been greater.

MASAYOSHI SON

**MASTER DEALMAKER:
FOUNDER, SOFTBANK**

When I was 19 years old, I saw a photo of a microprocessor in a science magazine for the first time. It was just a tiny chip that could fit on a fingertip but represented an entire computer. "Oh my God," I said to myself, "**this is going to change mankind's life.** This is the biggest invention that mankind ever created." And I started crying on the street. Those microprocessors were compacted into PCs, then linked together to create the internet and later smartphones. Now they are extending our knowledge and intelligence via artificial intelligence.

The industrial revolution transformed people's lives from the roots. But the information revolution is not just an extension of human capabilities but an extension of our brain cells. In a sense, our brains are more important than our arms and legs. This superintelligence will bring about developments we've never seen before and contribute to humanity.

Every morning I wake up and ask, Where am I? I don't know where I am because I am jumping around the world, but I don't want to go to sleep. It's thrilling.

MARTHA STEWART

AMERICAN TASTEMAKER: EPONYMOUS SEAL OF APPROVAL

There's no room for sloppiness, inaccuracy or omission when you're trying to build a relationship with a customer base. I'm very clear that everything I do is authentic, practiced and viable—and the end result is generally beautiful. I'm sure that's the same way Steve Jobs created his products.

125

RATAN TATA

**INDIA'S INDUSTRIALIST:
FORMER CHAIRMAN, TATA
MOTORS, TATA STEEL, TATA
CONSULTANCY SERVICES, ETC.**

Be passionate in areas relevant to
you, and **be a voice that is respected and abreast of developments.** I
have also tried not to express a view
on matters which I am not fully
involved with or qualified to comment upon.

DONALD TRUMP

SALESMAN AND RINGMASTER EXTRAORDINAIRE: OWNER, TRUMP ORGANIZATION; 45TH PRESIDENT OF THE UNITED STATES

The greatest business lesson I've learned in life is the same message I have for young people across America: Never give up. Even in the most difficult circumstances, have faith in yourself, confidence in your abilities and the conviction that you will be able to win for your family, for your business and for your country. But you have to relish the fight—**you have to enjoy coming in to work each day and going to battle for what you believe in,** and for the people who you believe in. And if you do that, if you keep moving forward, then each victory along the way will feed into another victory, and another opportunity, and another chance for a breakthrough.

By building this momentum, by pushing, by never backing down and by refusing to allow other people to define your limits, you will bring your goals into closer range, and you will accomplish them. America is a land of dreams, and if we chase those dreams with all of our hearts, then our country will be greater than ever before.

127

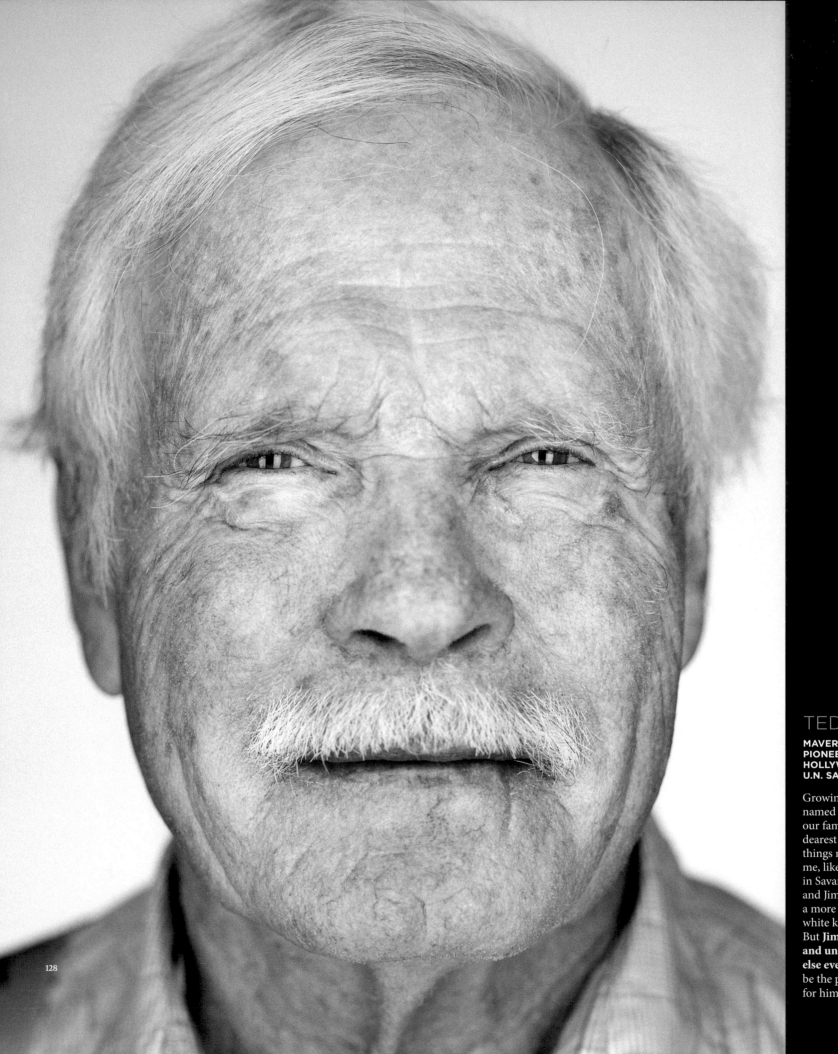

TED TURNER

MAVERICK: CABLE TELEVISION PIONEER; FOUNDER, CNN; HOLLYWOOD STUDIO DABBLER; U.N. SAVIOR

Growing up, my father hired a man named Jimmy Brown to work for our family, and he became one of my dearest friends. Jimmy taught me things my own father couldn't teach me, like how to sail. We were living in Savannah during segregation, and Jimmy and I couldn't have been a more unlikely pair—a privileged white kid and a grown black man. But **Jimmy provided more wisdom and understanding than anyone else ever did.** I don't think I would be the person I am today if it weren't for him.

HAMDI ULUKAYA

IMMIGRANT, RURAL JOBS CREATOR, BILLIONAIRE: FOUNDER, CHOBANI YOGURT

The poet Rumi wrote, "As you start to walk on the way, the way appears." When I started Chobani, I'd never run a company before and there was no plan. But one thing I saw that could be fixed easily was the factory's old walls: They badly needed a paint job. So I bought some paint, and our first five employees and I all got to work. It was the first and best decision I ever made. There's something magical in the movement, in the action—**it allows you to think, to discover new ideas and to feel like you're making progress.** So don't sit around waiting—act.

You cannot do everything alone—especially when you get to a certain level. It is impossible. I had to rely on myself and trust my decisions when it came to building Chobani—and today I still do. But we're a team made up of a lot of people who I'd trust with my life.

129

CRAIG VENTER

THE DECODER: FOUNDER, CELERA GENOMICS; HUMAN GENOME SEQUENCER; CHAIRMAN, HUMAN LONGEVITY INC. AND SYNTHETIC GENOMICS INC.

Timing is everything in science, like it is in most things in life. In 1944 Oswald Avery did the experiment proving DNA was how traits are inherited. But he didn't get the Nobel Prize because everybody wanted to believe proteins were the genetic material.

I've been lucky. I nearly flunked out of high school, and I decided not to go to college even though I had a swimming scholarship. I ended up in Vietnam. After, I had to start my education over from scratch. I had this English teacher, Bruce Cameron. We became lifelong friends. If it weren't for him, I would not have survived the first semester of community college. He taught me to ignore the assignment and write what I wanted. I ended up getting my Ph.D. in just three years.

I learned that **most people fail in science because they talk themselves out of doing the experiment.** Ideas are a dime a dozen. What makes the difference is the execution of the idea. That taught me to recognize when it was time to adopt new technologies to understand genetics and then even to sequence the human genome. Once, I was too early: I started trying to create synthetic life a decade before the world was ready for it. But it's ready now.

DIANE VON FURSTENBERG

FASHION ICON: ENTREPRENEUR, TASTEMAKER, INVENTOR OF THE WRAP DRESS

My mother, a Holocaust survivor, taught me that fear is not an option and that has been my guideline. I came to America in 1970 as a young European bride, with a dream and a suitcase full of Italian printed jersey dresses that I had designed. They were simple, easy, sexy little dresses that could be worn anywhere and did not wrinkle. My guardian angel mentor was Angelo Ferretti, the Italian man who owned the factory those dresses were made in. He believed in me, and I believed in his printed jersey fabric.

In New York I met my second mentor, the editor-in-chief of American *Vogue*, Diana Vreeland. Although I had shown my dresses to other editors, she saw something special in them, something modern and fresh. She helped me with exposure and introducing me to stores. With the help of a salesman, I took a showroom. Soon after, I designed the first wrap dress. Overnight that dress became a huge commercial success and a symbol of women's liberation. Soon we were making 25,000 dresses a week. I was living the American Dream and established my brand.

After that I had many ups and downs, but what allowed me to survive is that I was always honest and I truly believed in what I did. With my dress, **I was selling confidence and, with its success, I was getting more and more confident.** Confidence in what you do is crucial, but that does not mean being delusional. You must always face the truth and combat the obstacles as they appear.

132

SANDY WEILL

**WALL STREET CONGLOMERATOR:
SHEARSON, TRAVELERS, CITIGROUP**

I retired as CEO of Citigroup in 2003 and
retired as chairman in 2006 because I was
afraid of making an abrupt change in my
life. That turned out to be a mistake, as **I
should have retired from both positions
at the same time.** When you've been the
CEO of something for a long time and
you retire, you should really retire. As
chairman I spoke to directors about various issues and things that I thought were
wrong, and I felt I was sometimes getting
a response that they thought I wanted
my old job as CEO back. I stress the im-
portance of having another life outside of
business so that when it does come time
to retire, the transition is easier. For me
that other life has been in philanthropy for
the last four decades.

JACK WELCH

**THE CEO OF CEOS:
FORMER CEO, GE**

My biggest mistake was explosive—literally. In 1963, three years into my GE career, I was a chemical engineer, eager and ambitious and trying like hell to build a plastics business in an electrical company. In the process, my pilot plant blew up. Yes, blew up—roof collapsed, windows shattered, clouds of smoke, the works. I thank God no one was hurt, to this day. But I was certain my career was over, especially when my boss in Pittsfield suddenly didn't know me, and I got a call to go see the big boss in New York. His name was Charlie Reed, and I didn't know him at all. What I did know was that I was terrified—I was sure I was going to be yelled at, humiliated and then unceremoniously fired. After all, it was my plant and my fault.

But Charlie Reed taught me a huge lesson about leadership and life that day. He was calm. He was kind. He was thoughtful. He spent several hours with me, employing the Socratic method of questioning, to help me understand why the explosion occurred and what I could have—and could have—done differently. And then, after it was all over, he gave me a second chance.

I learned to never kick someone when they're down. Everyone makes mistakes, and **some are real whoppers. But that makes them whopping opportunities,** too—for growth. In the years after my encounter with Charlie, I followed his example with my own employees, and saw it help more people for the better. I also learned that the time to "kick" people—and by kick I mean "challenge"—is when they're on the way up, to remind them that when you're growing, make sure your head isn't swelling, too!

133

LES WEXNER

**MALL STORE JUGGERNAUT:
VISIONARY FOR THE LIMITED
(VICTORIA'S SECRET, PINK,
BATH & BODY WORKS, ETC.)**

Back when I had just a few stores, I made a cold call to the office of John Galbreath, who was probably the most successful guy in Ohio at the time. He was a big international real estate developer, but he also owned the Pittsburgh Pirates and had a private airport outside of Columbus, where the queen of England once flew in to talk to him about Thoroughbred horse breeding.

I introduced myself over the phone, and he invited me to his office. We talked for about an hour. What I really wanted to know was how he had gone from being a kid on a farm to a friend of the queen of England. He told me that the key was just to be curious and pursue various interests. Riding down the elevator, I remember sort of shaking my head and thinking to myself, what a load of crap. Here I had come for wisdom, and he just tells me to be curious.

And yet, I have continued to reflect on that conversation in the 40 years since then. Curiosity led me to see if I could replicate building one successful retail brand into creating several. I ended up building Victoria's Secret, Express, Abercrombie & Fitch and Bath & Body Works. Curiosity made me wonder if I could have success in picking the right garments for stores. Would I have an eye for picking out artwork? I eventually selected a collection centered on Pablo Picasso. If I was a leader in my business and industry, could I become a leader in my community, too? I now devote 10% to 20% of my time to improving my hometown of Columbus, Ohio. **Curiosity has kept me young as I have gotten older.** Now, nearly a half century after I walked into Galbreath's office, I'm still curious to see what's next.

134

MEG WHITMAN

CEILING BREAKER, COMPANY BUILDER: FORMER CEO, EBAY; CEO, HEWLETT PACKARD ENTERPRISE

There is a myth (at least I believe it's a myth) that being successful demands that we give up on decent, common-sense values: honesty, family, community, integrity, generosity, courage, empathy, etc. As we advance in our careers, there is this belief that winning at all costs is winning nonetheless. I never bought into that myth. **I respect ambition, but not ruthless ambition.**

We have the opportunity today to use our values to help us reinvent our future during a time of great stress and economic anxiety. There are those who see a focus on values as a luxury for prosperous times, when we can "afford" to think about making the world a kinder or nobler place. I want to make a different argument: It is precisely during difficult times that we need to align our priorities and actions with the fundamental principles that ultimately create stability, efficiency, energy and even prosperity. Navigating by essential values can have a force-multiplying effect.

OPRAH WINFREY

TALK SHOW MASTER; SYNDICATION SUPERSTAR; BRANDING JUGGERNAUT; FOUNDER, OPRAH WINFREY NETWORK

I was invited by Nelson Mandela to stay at his home for ten days. At first, I was very intimidated. I'd said to my partner Stedman, "What am I going to talk about for ten days and ten nights at Nelson Mandela's house?" And Stedman said, "Why don't you try listening?" So when I was there, halfway through my visit with him, I got comfortable sitting and being with him. First of all, when you go to Nelson Mandela's house, what do you take? You can't bring a candle. **What I wanted to do really was leave something that would be of value.** When we were talking one day, we started a conversation about what was in the newspaper: poverty and how to change it. And I said, "The only way to change poverty is through education, and one day I would like to build a school in South Africa." And he said, "You want to build a school?" He got up and called the minister of education. That afternoon I was in a meeting talking about building a school.

136

STEVE WYNN

KING OF THE STRIP: SAVIOR, GOLDEN NUGGET; FOUNDER, MIRAGE RESORTS, WYNN RESORTS, ETC.

I'm in the service business, where 10% of the franchise is the stuff and 90% is the guest experience. So the big question for me: How do you motivate employees? With 13,000 of them at the Wynn and Encore, you can't have 6,500 supervisors watching 6,500 people. You need to have a culture instead of a payroll, so that people watch themselves. What does this? Not money, but enhanced self-esteem.

Spotlight programs, such as Employee of the Month, are great, but there's honest prejudice built into them, as well as luck. So we retrained 1,300 supervisors to become something of a psychologist and learn how to evoke a story. Every day they hold 15-minute preshift meetings that start out like this: Who can tell us about something that happened yesterday with a guest? Then when staffers tell the story, we reinforce it. We thank them. The supervisor calls a storytelling hotline. We then put the story on the in-house internet and plaster it on the walls. **We make the storyteller a hero and do this hundreds of times a week.** Now I have 13,000 people looking for a story—it's the thing that brings them all together. Since the employees get to nominate themselves, they control their own enhanced self-esteem. That's the key to paradise.

137

138

TADASHI YANAI
FOUNDER, FAST RETAILING (UNIQLO)

I come from a small mining town in Ya-maguchi Prefecture. **My lifestyle is based on doing the right thing and on being correct in my actions.** In my daily life I try my best to practice what is known as Shin Zen Bi, which translates to Truth, Goodness, Beauty. By continuing with these values, I believe I can live my life in a reputable way.

MUHAMMAD YUNUS

**FATHER OF MICROLENDING:
FOUNDER, GRAMEEN BANK;
WINNER, NOBEL PEACE PRIZE**

Capitalism has been interpreted to be based on greed. But while human beings are selfish, they're also selfless. Why is the latter part discarded from the interpretation? We're increasingly seeing social businesses, or nondividend businesses, whose entire objective is to solve problems rather than make money, being born in many parts of the world. In social businesses, profits are recycled inside the company itself to continue work on a problem. Investors get to recoup their money but nothing more, other than the enjoyment of what they've done. **Making money is a happiness; making other people happy is a super-happiness.**

An example: We've started Grameen Shakti, or "Grameen Energy," to bring electricity to rural Bangladesh. We tell people, "Whatever money you spend on kerosene every month, give that money to us, and we'll give you electricity." And we use their money to finance their solar home system—and after three years, they get to keep it without any other payments. We've created 2 million solar-powered rural homes, the world's largest off-grid system, and customers can't believe it—they can now have television and charge mobile phones. It's so successful, many competitors have sprung up—which we welcome, because we are a social business, and those competitors help solve the problem.

In Bangladesh, for the last three years, we have been asking unemployed young people to come up with their own moneymaking business ideas, and we invest in them. We become the social business venture capital fund for them. We assure them that none of them will be rejected, only the implementation-ready ones will get funded. Now we fund 1,500 new entrepreneurs each month. This number keeps growing every month. Nineteen thousand businesses have already been funded. Success rate is 99.5%. We believe all human beings are born as entrepreneurs. They are not born to work for somebody else. Their early history is about being hunters, gatherers and problem-solvers. It remained as an essential part of our DNA; we are not job-seekers, we are job creators. Job-seeking is a wrong turn in our history.

139

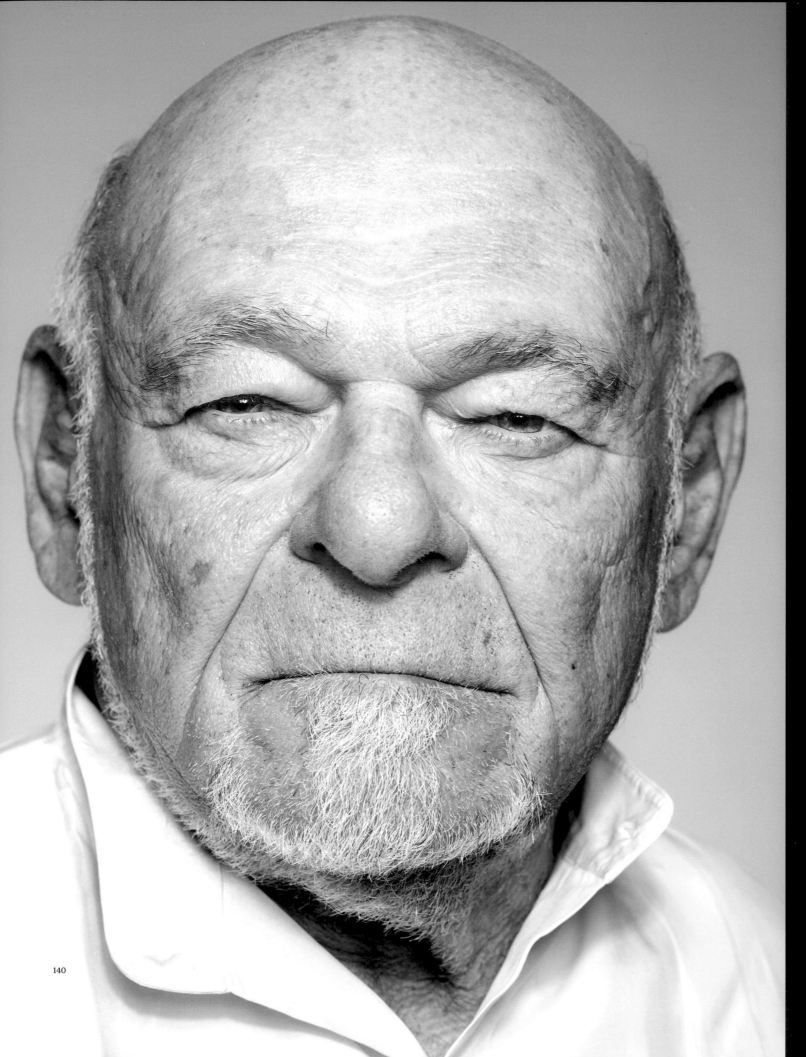

SAM ZELL

THE GRAVE DANCER: VULTURE LEGEND, REIT COLLECTOR

There were many times in my life when I would have liked to follow the herd. Instead, **I have always followed my gut—and sometimes it's been really lonely.** In 1991, I was standing in the lobby of a bank, and they had agreed to sell me an office building at 50 cents on the dollar. I kept looking over my shoulder and wondering why there were not all sorts of people waiting in line behind me. After all, this was an incredible opportunity. Maybe I was wrong? But I thought it through again and decided that I knew what I was doing, so I kept going. By 1994 all those people were there in line, but the bulk of the opportunity had passed. When you look at The Forbes 400 list and take off everybody who inherited money, what's left are people who went right when everyone else went left. Conventional wisdom leads to mediocrity.

140

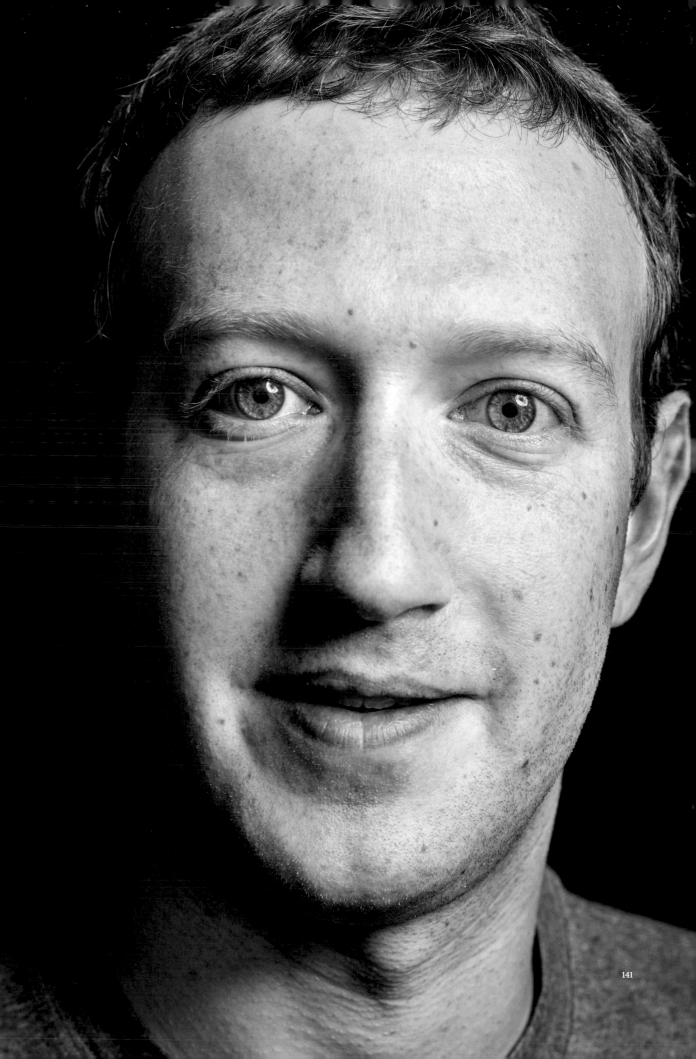

MARK ZUCKERBERG

**GLOBAL CONNECTOR:
COFOUNDER, FACEBOOK**

My hope was never to build a company. I was driven by a sense of purpose to connect people and bring us closer together.

A couple years after starting Facebook, some big companies wanted to buy us. Nearly everyone else wanted to sell, but I didn't. I wanted to see if we could connect more people. It tore our company apart, fraying relationships until, within a year or so, every single person on the management team was gone.

That was my hardest time leading Facebook. I believed in what we were doing, but I felt alone. And worse, it was my fault. It taught me that it's not enough to have purpose yourself. You have to create a sense of purpose for others. And I hadn't explained what I hoped to build.

That sense of purpose creates motivation and meaning for people beyond just surviving or making money. It attracts other people who are interested in the right things. People here build products because they want to do something meaningful and play an important part in how people use Facebook. The company has to be successful for us to keep going, but the real motivation is creating positive social change in the world.

I think that's true for most good businesses. Building something like Facebook and running a community like ours requires some aspiration. A lot of our leadership team is wired that way. Our compass as a company is all about making our services available to the most people possible so we can give everyone around the world a voice.

People often ask me for advice about starting a company, and I always tell them **your goal should never be starting a company. Focus on the change you want to make,** find people who share your same purpose, and eventually you may have an opportunity to build something that helps create purpose for others and has a positive impact on the world.

141

"Business was originated to produce happiness, not to pile up millions."

—B.C. FORBES